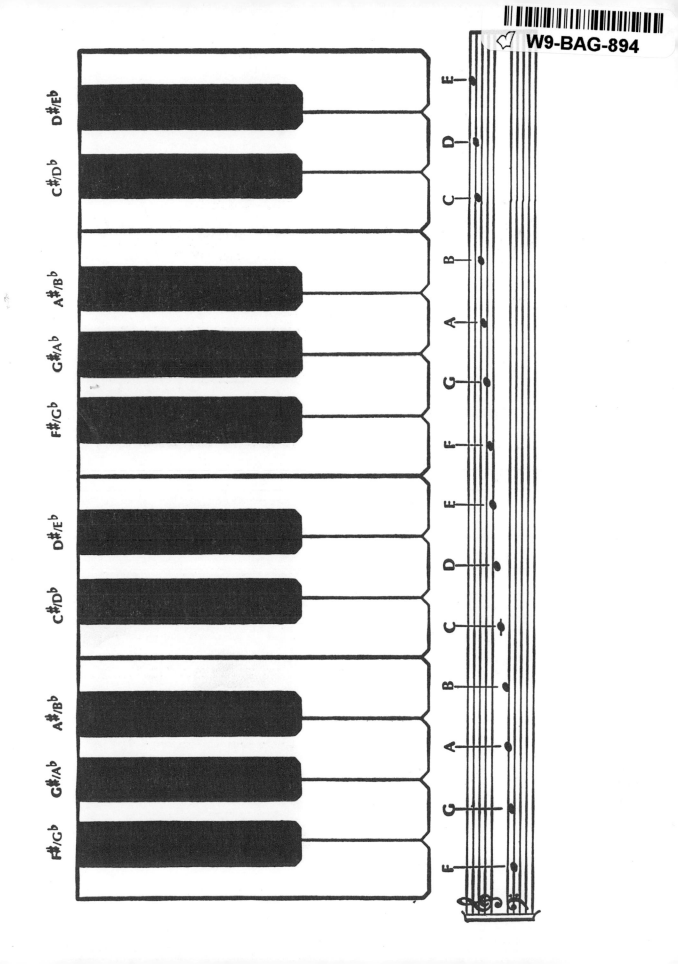

THE Music CONNECTION

PROGRAM AUTHORS

Jane Beethoven
Dulce Bohn
Patricia Shehan Campbell
Carmen E. Culp
Jennifer Davidson
Lawrence Eisman
Sandra Longoria Glover
Charlotte Hayes

Martha Hilley
Mary E. Hoffman
Hunter March
Bill McCloud
Marvelene Moore
Catherine Nadon-Gabrion
Mary Palmer
Carmino Ravosa

Mary Louise Reilly
Will Schmid
Carol Scott-Kassner
Jean Sinor
Sandra Stauffer
Judith Thomas

RECORDING PRODUCERS

Darrell Bledsoe
Jeanine Levenson

J. Douglas Pummill
Buryl Red, Executive Producer

Linda Twine
Ted Wilson

SILVER BURDETT GINN

MORRISTOWN, NJ   NEEDHAM, MA

Atlanta, GA   Dallas, TX   Deerfield, IL   Menlo Park, CA

ISBN 0-382-26182-8

C·O·N·T

·E·N·T·S

THEME MUSICAL

READING 212

REFERENCE BANK

CONCEPTS

Music!
What do you think of when you hear that word?

Do you think of melody? Rhythm?
Harmony? Form?

Do you think of how instruments and voices
sound?

Melody, rhythm, harmony, form,
and the sounds of instruments and voices
are music concepts.

The first section of your book will help you learn

about concepts, or ideas, in music.

Music is yours to enjoy.
The more you know about it,
the more you will love it.

section 1

The BEAT Goes on

Some children keep a steady beat by moving.

Move to the steady beat as you sing or listen.

Zudio

Traditional American Street Song

Here we go zu - di - o, zu - di - o, zu - di - o,

Here we go zu - di - o, all night long. —

Step back, Sal - ly, Sal - ly, Sal - ly, Step back, Sal - ly, all night long. —

Walkin' down the alley, what do I see?
I see a great big man from Tennessee.
Betcha five dollars I can catch that man,
Betcha five dollars I can catch that man.
To the side, to the side, to the side, side, side;
To the side, to the side, to the side, side, side,
Side, side, side.

My mama called the doctor; the doctor said,
   (Verse 1) "Oo, oh, I got a pain in my head."
     (Verse 2) "Oo, oh, I got a pain in my tum."
      (Verse 3) "Oo, oh, I got a pain in my side."
To the side, to the side, to the side, side, side;
To the side, to the side, to the side, side, side,
Side, side, side.

Do a Shimmy Shake

You can do a "shimmy shake" dance to this song.

Find a partner to learn the dance with.

Down, Down, Baby

African American Clapping Song

Down, down, ba - by, down, _ down a rol - ler coast - er,

Sweet, sweet ba - by, I ____ love a rol - ler coast - er;

Shim - my, shim - my, co - coa pop, shim - my, shim - my, pop, ___

All to - geth – er with the chick-ens and the feath - ers.

P – O – P spells pop, oh, my hon – ey,

P – O – P spells pop, oh, my ba – by,

P – O – P spells POP!

Spring Comes, Winter Goes

Winter in Japan is very cold. There is a lot of snow.
Children in Japan sing a song when spring comes.
Birds sing and cherry blossoms bloom.

Children in Snow   *Hiroshi Hamaya-Magnum*

Springtime Has Come (Haru Nga Kita)

English Words by Patty Zeitlin   *Folk Song from Japan*

1. Spring - time has come, oh, spring - time has come, oh,
2. Flow - ers are bloom - ing, Flow - ers are bloom - ing,
3. Birds are a - sing - ing, Birds are a - sing - ing,

How do you know it's true? _____
Where are ___ they in bloom? _____
Where can we hear them sing? _____

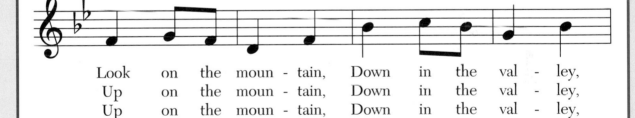

Look on the moun - tain, Down in the val - ley,
Up on the moun - tain, Down in the val - ley,
Up on the moun - tain, Down in the val - ley,

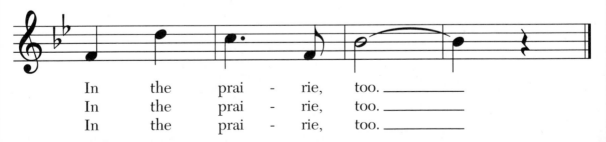

In the prai - rie, too. _____
In the prai - rie, too. _____
In the prai - rie, too. _____

Sing and Move

There are two patterns in this song.
Can you tell what they are?

Shake Hands, Mary

African-American Children's Song

1. Shake hands, Mar - y, Dum-a - la - lum. _
2. Strut, ___ Ma - ry, Dum-a - la - lum. _
3. Dance, ___ Ma - ry, Dum-a - la - lum. _

Shake hands, Mar - y, Dum-a - la - lum. _
Strut, ___ Ma - ry, Dum-a - la - lum. _
Dance, ___ Ma - ry, Dum-a - la - lum. _

REFRAIN

Lum, lum, lum, lum, Dum-a - la - lum. _

Lum, lum, lum, lum, Dum-a - la - lum. _

"March" from *The Nutcracker* ....Tchaikovsky

Sounds Around Us

Look at the pictures.

Imagine that they can make sounds.
Describe the sounds you "hear."
Use the words below to help you.

high	low	fast	slow
loud	soft	long	short

Music Around Us

Listen to the music on the recording.
Point to the word that matches the sounds you hear.

LONG

short

fast

SLOW

HIGH

LOW

loud

soft

13

Kites

Go Upward and Downward

Kites go upward and kites go downward.
All they need is a good puff of wind.
Have you ever flown a kite?
Wasn't it fun!

Let's Go Fly a Kite

Words and Music by Richard M. Sherman and Robert B. Sherman

Let's go fly a kite Up to the high - est height!

Let's go fly a kite And send it soar - ing

Up through the at - mos - phere,

Up where the air is clear.

Oh, let's go _____ fly a kite! _____

The Stars Run Down

Listen for notes going upward in this song.
Listen for notes going downward.

Oh, Watch the Stars

Folk Song from South Carolina

Oh, watch the stars, see how they run.

Oh, watch the stars, see how they run. _____

The _ stars run down _____ at the set-ting of the sun.

Oh, watch the stars, see how they run.

Find an instrument with wooden or metal bars. Take out all the bars except these.

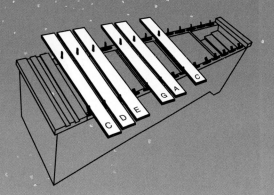

You can play this pattern with the song.

C D E G A C A G

C A G E C D C

Spider Web.............Diamond

INTRODUCING THE
FROG

Listen to the recording of this song before you sing it.
What happens before the song begins?
How does it help to introduce the song?

Frogs

English Words by Betty Warner Dietz and Thomas Choonbai Park   *Folk Song from China*

Each frog has a sin-gle mouth. He has two eyes and four legs.

Pin pong pin pong, Count them with me. Dur-ing time of peace frogs do not drink.

Dur-ing time of peace frogs do not drink. Wa-ter lil-ies float on the pond.

Wa-ter lil-ies float on the pond.

Da Ruan

Er Hu

Yang Qin

Ba Wu

Fishermen's Song
.... Traditional Chinese

Beginnings and Endings

This song has an introduction on the recording.
Does it help you begin at the right place?
What happens at the end of the song?

Shake Them 'Simmons Down

Play-Party Song from Texas

1. Cir - cle right, do - oh, do - oh,

Cir - cle right, do - oh, do - oh,

Cir - cle right, do - oh, do - oh,

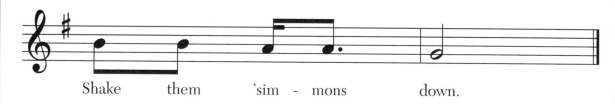

Shake them 'sim - mons down.

2. Circle left, do-oh, do-oh,
   Circle left, do-oh, do-oh,
   Circle left, do-oh, do-oh,
   Shake them 'simmons down.

3. Boys to the center, do-oh, do-oh, . . .

4. Girls to the center, do-oh, do-oh, . . .

5. Promenade all, do-oh, do-oh, . . .

6. Swing your corner, do-oh, do-oh, . . .

Play Me Some Fiddle (excerpt)
...........Daniels

String Sounds

Hampton University Museum, Hampton VA.

The Banjo Lesson   *Henry Ossawa Tanner*

String instruments make many different sounds.
Listen, then describe the sounds that you hear.

Old Joe Clark...........Traditional

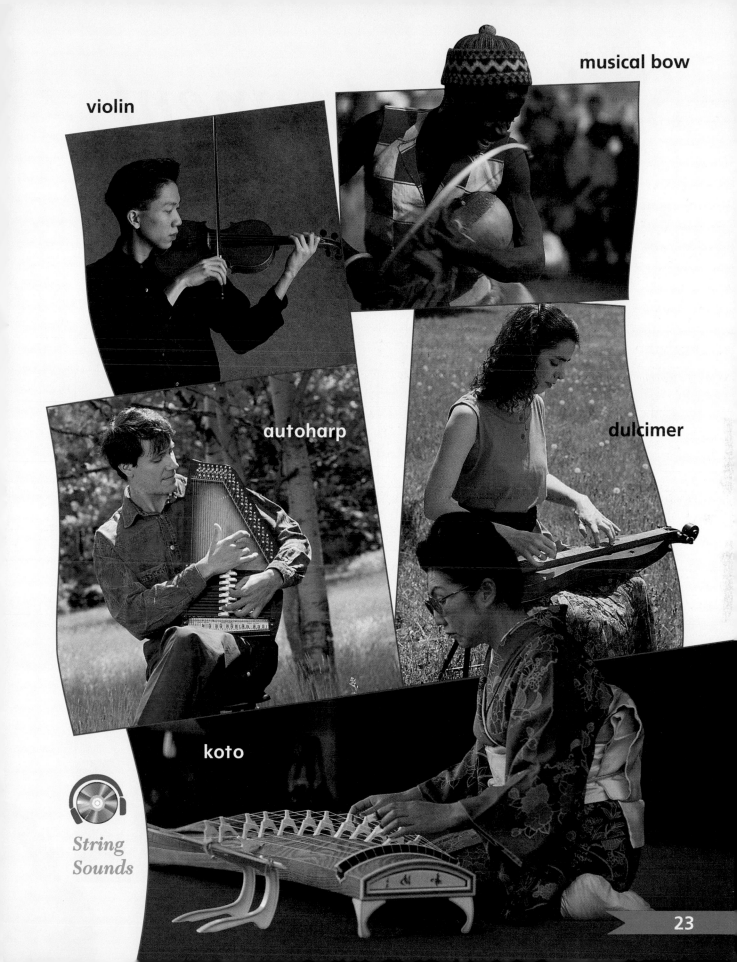

violin

musical bow

autoharp

dulcimer

koto

String
Sounds

23

Making a
String Instrument

1 Listen to the sound of a string instrument in this piece. Which string instrument do you think it is?

2 Hold a rubber band between your hands.

Pluck the rubber band.

How does it sound?

3 Try to make the sound louder. Here is one idea.

Use a tissue box.

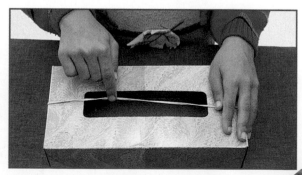

4 You can make a *diddley bow*.

Try to play the diddley bow as shown here.

5

Listen to the sound of a diddley bow.

Shake 'Em On Down ....Jones

Styles
in Music

Pretend to play
the guitar in two
different ways.

Which has the
strongest beat?

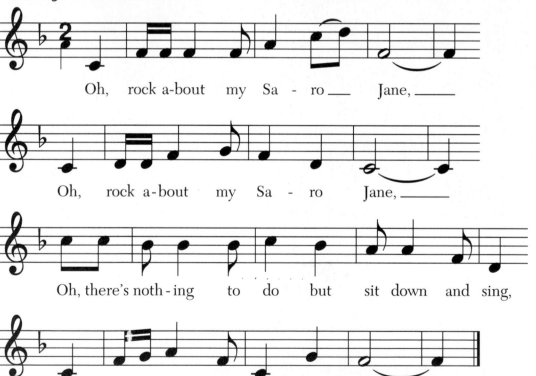

Rock About My Saro Jane
Folk Song from the United States

Oh,   rock a-bout   my   Sa - ro ___   Jane, ___

Oh,   rock a-bout   my   Sa - ro   Jane, ___

Oh, there's noth-ing   to   do   but   sit down   and   sing,

And   rock a-bout   my   Sa - ro   Jane. ___

Rock version of "Rock About My Saro Jane"

A Tall Tale

These drawings show the two sections in "Old Dan Tucker."

 A **B**

Do you think the sections will sound the same or different? Why?

Old Dan Tucker

Folk Song from the United States

A

1. Old Dan Tuck-er was a might-y man,

He washed his face in the fry-ing pan,

Combed his hair with a wag-on wheel,

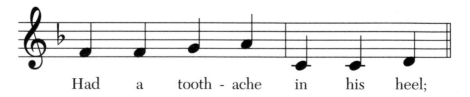

Had a tooth-ache in his heel;

REFRAIN

So get out the way, Old Dan Tuck-er;

Get out the way, Old Dan Tuck-er;

Get out the way, Old Dan Tuck-er,

You're too late to get your sup-per.

2. Old Dan Tucker came to town,
   Riding a billy goat, leading a hound;
   Hound dog barked, then billy goat jumped;
   Dan fell off and landed on a stump; *Refrain*

Can you make up some other words about Dan Tucker?

Bounce and Catch

Show the beat by bouncing and catching a ball.

One, Two, Three, Alary
Playground Chant

1. One, two, three, a - lar - y,
2. One, two, three, a - lar - y,
3. One, two, three, a - lar - y,

My first name is Mar - y.
I saw Pe - ter Ter - ry
Lost my new ca - na - ry,

If you think it nec - es - sar - y,
Sit - ting on a bum - ble - ber - ry,
When you find him, call him Bar - ry,

Look it up in the dic - tion - ar - y.
Eat - ing lots of de - li - cious cher - ries.
One, ____ two, _____ three, a - lar - y.

From *Sally Go Round the Sun* by Edith Fowke. Reprinted by permission of the author.

Bounce your ball to this pattern.

Listen to this music.
Does it remind you of a ball
in motion?

"The Ball"
from *Children's Games*
.............Bizet

Rhythm Patterns to Play

How many rhythm patterns can you find in this song?

How Good and Joyous

Hebrew Folk Song

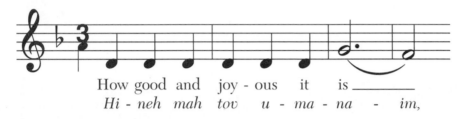

How good and joy - ous it is _____
Hi - neh mah tov u - ma - na - im,

For broth - ers to dwell to - geth - er.
She - vet a - chim gam ya - chad.

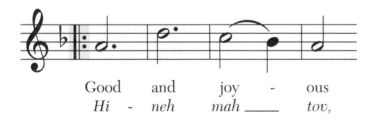

Good and joy - ous
Hi - neh mah _____ tov,

For broth - ers to dwell to - geth - er.
She - vet a - chim gam ya - chad.

Play these patterns with the song.

KEEP THE BEAT

Listen for the nonsense words in this song.

Waddaly Atcha

Words and Music by Kassel-Stitzel

Wad - da - ly a - tcha, wad - da - ly a - tcha,

Doo - dle-ee - doo, _ doo - dle-ee - doo; _

Wad - da - ly a - tcha, wad - da - ly a - tcha,

Doo - dle-ee - doo, _ doo - dle-ee - doo; _

You can do a hand-jive with "Waddaly Atcha."
See the motions below.

It's the sim - pl-est thing, _ noth - in' much to ___ it, ___

All you got to do is doo - dle - ee - doo it; ___

I like the rest, _ But the part I love best, _

It goes doo - dle-ee, doo - dle - ee - doo. Whoo!

In Harmony with Africa

Mask of a Mythic Royal Ancestor   *Kuba People*

Listen to the song from Nigeria.
What do you hear the voices doing?
When do you hear only one voice?
When do you hear many voices?

Ise Oluwa

Yoruba Folk Song from Nigeria

I - se ____ o - lu - wa ____ ko le ba - je - oh; ____

Last time sing 3 times.

Fine

I - se ____ o - lu - wa ____ ko le ba - je - oh. ____

D.C. al Fine

Ko le ba - je - oh, ____ ko le ba - je - oh. ____

© 1989 Nitanju Bolade Casel (Clear Ice Music)

Making Harmony

You can play an autoharp with this song.

The chord names in the boxes tell you which buttons to push as you strum.

"Invocation of the Powerful Spirits" from *Panambé*
..............Ginastera

Lullaby, My Jamie

Words by Rose Stanfield   *Folk Song from Latvia*

1. Lul - la - by, my Ja - mie,
2. Snow-white lambs for Ja - mie,

Soft - ly sleep, my child,
All kinds for your own,

Sis - ter gent - ly rocks you,
Cur - ly, bob - tailed, long - tailed,

Light her hands and mild.
When a man you're grown.

Saying Goodbye

You can play the autoharp with this song, too. Which chords will you play?

Go Well and Safely

English Words by Olcutt Sanders   Zulu Parting Song

Go   well ___ and   safe - ly,
Ham - ba - ni   kah - le,

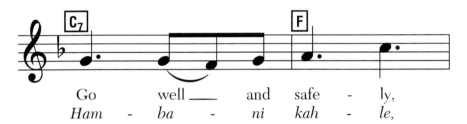

Go   well ___ and   safe - ly,
Ham - ba - ni   kah - le,

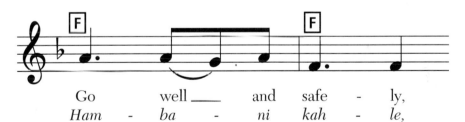

Go   well ___ and   safe - ly,
Ham - ba - ni   kah - le,

The   Lord   be   ev - er   with   you. ___
I   nkoni   ma - yi - be   na - ni. _____

Finding a Pattern

Old John Braddelum

Words Adapted   Folk Melody from England

1. Num - ber one, Num - ber one,

Now my song has just be - gun.

Look for this short-short-long pattern in the song.

How many times do you see it?

With a rum-tum tad-de-lum, Old John Brad-de-lum,

Hey, what hap - py folk are we!

2. Number two, Number two,
   You're with me and I'm with you.
   Refrain

3. Number three, Number three,
   This is easy as can be.
   Refrain

4. Number four, Number four,
   Just keep singing—we want more!
   Refrain

5. Number five, Number five,
   It's so great to be alive!
   Refrain

Listen for the tambourine in this music.
Which set of lines below
shows the pattern it plays?

1 _ _ __   2 __ _ _

Staines Morris Dance (excerpt) ....Anonymous

SHORT and LONG SOUNDS

It is a sunny day.
Chickens, ducklings and geese
come out to play.

In the Barnyard

Words by Dorothy Aldis   Music by Milton Kaye

In __ the barn-yard   chick-ens walk,

They   jerk __ their heads. and   peck _ and   talk

While   yel-low duck-lings   run   a-round

From "In the Barnyard" by Dorothy Aldis, reprinted by permission of G. P. Putnam's Sons from HOP, SKIP AND JUMP!, copyright 1934, copyright renewed © 1961 by Dorothy Aldis.

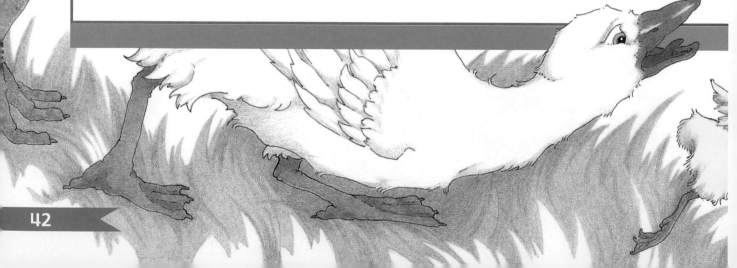

Show the long and short movements of the animals.

Chickens	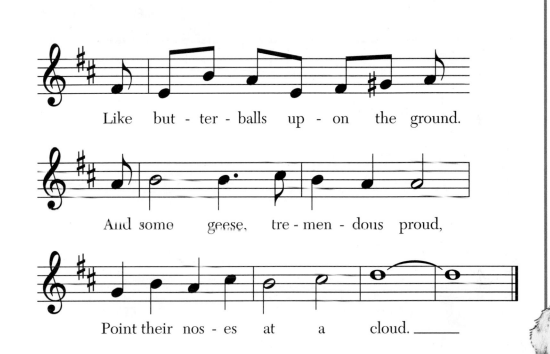	quarter notes
Ducklings		eighth notes
Geese		half notes

Like but - ter - balls up - on the ground.

And some geese, tre - men - dous proud,

Point their nos - es at a cloud. _____

Move to the short and longer sounds in this music.

"Ballet of the Unhatched Chicks" from *Pictures at an Exhibition*............Mussorgsky

RHYTHMS FOR THE Setting Sun

Native American children take part
in the songs and dances of their nation.

At an early age they learn
how to beat a drum or play a flute.

They also learn to shake rattles.

Sunset

Native American Song

Now the moon ___ is in the sky,

To the sun ___ we say good-bye;

Fa - ther Sun sleeps in the West.

From *Music for Young Americans* © 1959 American Book Company. Reprinted by permission of D. C. Heath and Company.

Play the steady beat on a tom-tom.

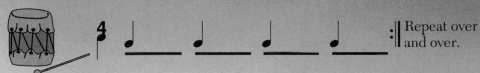

Repeat over and over.

Add these parts when you can.

Repeat over and over.

Repeat over and over.

Snake Dance ....Native American

In the sky _____ we see the moon;

Shad-ows creep, ___ the night comes soon;

Fa-ther Sun sleeps in the West,

And his peo-ple go to ___ rest.

One Voice Many Voices

When one person sings, it is a solo. When many people sing, it is a chorus.

Michael, Row the Boat Ashore

African American Work Song

Solo

1. Mich - ael, row the boat a - shore,

Chorus

Hal - le - lu - jah!

Solo

Mich - ael, row the boat a - shore,

Chorus

Hal - le - lu - jah!

2. Noah was a gentle man, . . .

3. Gabriel, blow the trumpet strong, . . .

4. Brother, help me turn the wheel, . . .

*Bamnqobile
......Shabalala*

Little Boy Song

Calypso from Trinidad

VERSE

Solo

I am a little { boy / girl } from Trinidad,

Sometimes I am good, sometimes I am bad.

Mama she talk, talk all the day

How I should grow up and how I should play.

REFRAIN

Chorus

Keep out of fire, ___ you will get burned, -

Keep out of fire, ___ you will get burned; -

I don't be - lieve her, ___ try to de - ceive her, ___

No more play with fire ___ I have learned.

From LITTLE CALYPSOS by Lillian D. Krugman and Alice Jeanne Ludwig; published by PERIPOLE, Browns Mills, NJ

Step, Leap, and Repeat...

In this song a cowhand tells about life on the trail.

Lone Star Trail
Cowboy Song from the United States

1. I start-ed on the trail on June twen-ty-third,

I been punch-in' Tex-as cat-tle on the Lone Star Trail;

REFRAIN

Sing-in' ki yi yip-pi yip-pi yay, yip-pi yay!

Sing-in' ki yi yip-pi yip-pi yay! _____

2. I'm up in the mornin' before daylight,
   And before I sleep the moon shines bright. *Refrain*

3. Oh, it's bacon and beans 'most every day,
   I'd as soon be a-eatin' prairie hay. *Refrain*

4. My feet are in the stirrups and my rope is on the side,
   Show me a horse that I can't ride. *Refrain*

Melodies can move by

step

leap

repeat

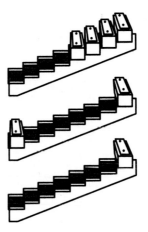

A Mix Up Charles M. Russel

1910, oil on canvas, 30 x 48. The Rockwell Museum, Corning, NY (78.54F)
Photo by Charles Swain.

Step, Leap, and Repeat...Latin Style

My Twenty Pennies

English Words by J. Olcutt Sanders   Folk Song from Venezuela

1. With twen - ty pen - nies, with twen - ty pen - nies,

With twen - ty pen - nies I bought a *pa - va.*

The *pa - va* had a *pa - vi - to,*

I have the *pa - va* and the *pa - vi - to;*

And so I still have my twen - ty pen - nies.

Repeat for additional lines in verses 2–6.

2. With twenty pennies, with twenty pennies,
   With twenty pennies I bought a *gata.*
   The *gata* had a *gatito,*
   I have the *gata* and the *gatito;*
   I have the *pava* and the *pavito;*
   And so I still have my twenty pennies.

3. . . . *chiva* . . . *chivito* . . .

4. . . . *mona* . . . *monito* . . .

5. . . . *lora* . . . *lorito* . . .

The Flute Steps Out

Listen to this music by Vivaldi.

Follow the steps, leaps, and repeats on the chart as you listen.

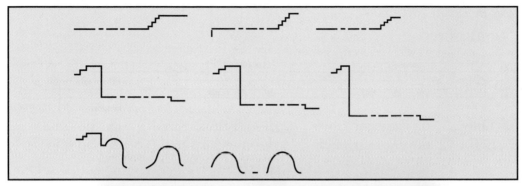

The Flute Player   *Judith Leyster*

NM 1120. *Photo:* SKM, The National Art Museums of Sweden, Stockholm

"Largo" from *Concerto for Flute in G Minor*.............Vivaldi

DINO LOUD,

Counting Up the Dinosaur

Words and Music by David Eddleman

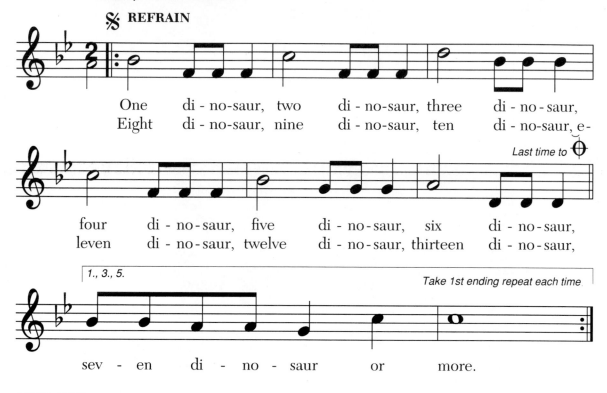

REFRAIN

One   di - no-saur, two   di - no-saur, three   di - no - saur,
Eight   di - no-saur, nine   di - no-saur, ten   di - no-saur, e-

Last time to

four   di - no-saur, five   di - no - saur, six   di - no - saur,
leven   di - no-saur, twelve   di - no - saur, thirteen   di - no - saur,

1., 3., 5.

Take 1st ending repeat each time

sev - en   di - no - saur   or   more.

2., 4., 6.

See a pte - ro - dac - tyl soar,
Hear the al - lo - sau - rus roar.
Bron - to - saur ga - lore,

1. Counting up the dinosaur is risky,
   Some may have a kingsize appetite;
   And when you are counting, don't get frisky,
   You could make a small but healthy bite for *Refrain*

2. When you saddle up a stegosaurus,
   When you are atop a reptile hide,
   Better keep the fellow's mouth in focus,
   You may finish up the ride inside of *Refrain*

3. Take a dino for a picnic outing,
   better wear a shiny cast-iron shirt;
   For you never know when he is scouting
   for a people-type to be dessert for *Refrain and Coda*

CODA

four-teen di - no-saur, fif-teen di - no - saur or more. ___

Do-Si Dinosaur ....Paleo-Yolen

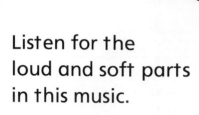

DANCING WITH

Listen for the loud and soft parts in this music.

The Dinosaur Dance

Words and Music by Ned Ginsburg

VERSES

1. Thousands and thousands of years ago,
   dinosaurs ruled the land.
   They plodded through their humdrum lives,
   and snow and mud and sand!
   But ev'ry once in a while,
   even dinosaurs need some fun.
   So they'd throw themselves a party
   right out in the scorching sun!
   And to this day,
   we celebrate the dinosaur way: *Refrain*

2. You don't need fancy dancin' shoes,
   don't strut your stylish stuff.
   Just do like a stegosaurus,
   that's sure to be enough!
   And don't make fun of your neighbor,
   'cause he's liable to chew you out!
   Just join in the jumpin' madness,
   that's what it's all about.
   Now, once again,
   you got to get ready, my friend: *Refrain*

REFRAIN

Lift your di-no-saur knee,   wig-gle your di-no-saur toes,

raise your di-no-saur hand,   and touch your di-no-saur nose.

© 1991 Ned Ginsburg

Dinosaur Tango ....Kassirer and Marcus

A *Fast* – and – *Slow* Game

What happens to the beat in this song?

Does it get faster?   Does it get slower?

Kee-Chee

Game from Zaire

Ah   wu - ne   ku - ne   cha   o   wu - ni,

Ah   wu - ne   ku - ne   cha   o   wu - ni;

Ah   yi   yi   ye - ki   ay   kae   ay - na,

Ah   yi   yi   ye - ki   ay   kae   ay - na;

A   oo _____ ah   dee   mee   kee - chee.

From "Girl Scout Pocket Songbook." Copyright 1956 Girl Scouts of the U.S.A.

THE PARTS OF THE TRAIN

This song has two different sections, (A) and B.
Which pattern on the train shows the form of the song?

Get on Board

African American Spiritual

(A) Get on board, lit-tle chil-dren,

Get on board, lit-tle chil-dren,

Get on board, lit-tle chil-dren,

There's room for man-y-a more.

B The gos-pel train's a-com-ing,

I hear it close at hand, ____

I hear the car-wheels rum-bling

And roll-ing through the land.

Ⓐ Get on board, lit-tle chil-dren,

Get on board, lit-tle chil-dren,

Get on board, lit-tle chil-dren,

There's room for man-y - a more.

Minuet in G

A minuet is a stately dance in ABA form. Move with a partner during section A. Move by yourself during section B.

Minuet in G
..........Beethoven

ABOUT THE MUSIC

Minuet in G was written by Ludwig van Beethoven (LOOD vihg van BAY toh v'n). In his day the minuet was a popular dance at court.

Listen to the graceful sounds of Beethoven's music. Imagine the people dancing in their beautiful clothes. Try to keep that feeling when you dance to the music.

Tapping Toes in Twos

Sing and dance to "Jubilee!"

Jubilee!

Singing Game from Kentucky

1. All out on the old rail-road, All out on the sea;

All out on the old rail-road, Far as eye can see.

REFRAIN

Swing an' turn, Ju-bi-lee! Live an' learn, Ju-bi-lee!

2. Hardest work I've ever done,
   Workin' on the farm;
   Easiest work I've ever done,
   Swingin' my true love's arm! *Refrain*

3. If I had me a needle and thread,
   Fine as I could sew,
   Sew my true love to my side,
   And down this creek I'd go. *Refrain*

4. If I had no horse to ride,
   I'd be found a-crawlin',
   Up and down this rocky road,
   Looking for my darlin'. *Refrain*

5. All out on the old railroad,
   All out on the sea;
   All out on the old railroad,
   Far as eye can see. *Refrain*

Circus Band Music ....Ives

1918
RINGLING BROS.
WORLD'S GREATEST
SHOWS
GRAND SPECTACLE
MAGAZINE &
DAILY REVIEW
PRICE 15 CENTS

Rabbit's Ears Are Grouped in Twos

Rabbit

Folk Song from Japan

Oh, Rab - bit, jump - ing free,

Tell me, Rab - bit, what you see.

"When I look up in - to the sky, ___

Moon is there; here _ am I." _____

Play steady beats on a woodblock.

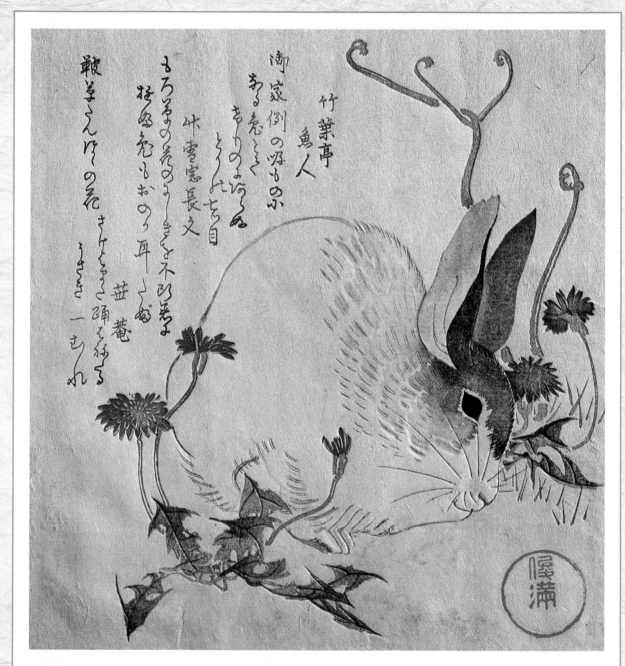

Rabbit *Japanese Woodblock Print*

Listen to this piece of music.

Can you hear how the beats are grouped?

 Stars and Stripes Forever (excerpt) ....Sousa

Sometimes It's the Same

What patterns can you find that repeat?

Little Wheel A-Turnin'

African American Spiritual

1. There's a lit-tle wheel a-turn-in' in my heart,

There's a lit-tle wheel a-turn-in' in my heart;

In my heart, _____ in my heart. _____

There's a lit-tle wheel a-turn-in' in my heart.

2. There's a little song a-singin' in my heart, . . .

3. There's a little love a-livin' in my heart, . . .

4. There's a little bell a-ringin' in my heart, . . .

5. There's a little drum a-beatin' in my heart, . . .

Does any part of the melody repeat in the song?

 River Run (excerpt)..........Glass

A Pattern of Surprises

Have you ever had a surprise?

In this song a surprise comes from a root.
Can you discover what the surprise is?

From a Lovely Root

English Words by Elizabeth S. Bachman   *Yiddish Folk Song*

1. From a love-ly root in the glen

Came a fine and love-ly tree.

Tree from the root;   Root in the glen;

So it is now and ev-er has been.

2. On the tree that came from the root
   Grew a fine and lovely branch.
   Branch on the tree;
   Tree from the root;
   Root in the glen;
   So it is now and ever has been.

3. On the branch that grew on the tree
   Sat a fine and lovely nest.
   Nest on the branch

4. In the nest that sat on the branch
   Sang a fine and lovely bird.
   Bird in the nest . . .

5. On the bird that sang in the nest
   Grew some fine and lovely feathers.
   Feathers on the bird . . .

6. From the lovely feathers on the bird
   Came a fine and lovely pillow.
   Pillow from the feathers . . .

SO MANY

Can you see repeated patterns in this picture?

THINGS REPEAT

What do you hear that repeats in this song?

Abiyoyo
Folk Lullaby from Africa

A - bi - yo - yo, _____ a - bi - yo - yo, _____

A - bi - yo - yo, _____ a - bi - yo - yo; _____

A - bi - yo - yo, bi - yo - yo, bi - yo - yo, _____

A - bi - yo - yo, bi - yo - yo, bi - yo - yo. _____

Abiyoyo ....African folk tale as told by Pete Seeger

Sounds of CARNIVAL

There is a special festival in Brazil.
It is called *carnival.*
As you listen to "Mama Paquita," listen for
the special sounds of the instruments.

Mama Paquita

English Words by Margaret Marks   *Carnival Song from Brazil*

1. Ma - ma Pa - qui - ta,   Ma - ma Pa - qui - ta,

Ma - ma Pa - qui - ta, buy your ba - by a pa - pa - ya,
Ma - ma Pa - qui - ta says, "I have-n't an - y mon-ey

A ripe pa - pa - ya   and a ba - na - na,
To buy pa - pa - yas   and ripe ba - na - nas,

1.
A ripe ba - na - na that your ba - by will en - joy, ma-ma-ma-ma,

Let's go to Car - ni -val and dance the night a - way!"

2. Mama Paquita, Mama Paquita,
   Mama Paquita, buy your baby some pajamas,
   Some new pajamas, a yellow blanket,
   A yellow blanket that your baby will enjoy, ma-ma-ma-ma.
   Mama Paquita, Mama Paquita,
   Mama Paquita says, "I haven't any money
   To buy pajamas, a yellow blanket,
   Let's go to Carnival and dance the night away!"

The Sound of Falling Rain

Weather

Dot a dot dot   dot a dot dot
Spotting the windowpane.
Spack a spack speck   flock a flack fleck
Freckling the windowpane.

A spatter a scatter   a wet cat a clatter
A splatter a rumble outside.
Umbrella umbrella umbrella umbrella
Bumbershoot barrel of rain.

Slosh a galosh   slosh a galosh
Slither and slather a glide
A puddle a jump a puddle a jump
A puddle a jump puddle splosh
A juddle a pump aluddle a dump a
Puddmuddle jump in and slide!

Eve Merriam

Can you add rain sounds to this song?
How will you begin and end it?

If All the Raindrops

Musical Arrangement by Sharon, Lois and Bram

If all the rain - drops were lem - on drops and gum drops,

Oh, what a rain it would be.

I'd stand out-side with my mouth o - pen wide;

I would - n't care if I nev - er went in - side.

If all the rain - drops were lem - on drops and gum drops,

Oh, what a rain it would be.

What sounds does the song tell about?
Listen for them on the recording.

The SOUND of a BELL

Temple Bell

Words from a Chinese Poem   *Melody from China*
Adapted by Burton Kurth

1. Moun-tains hid in a mist-y cloud;

Bam-boos lin-ing the dust-y road.

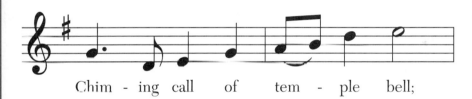

Chim-ing call of tem-ple bell;

Night is fall-ing on field and dell.

2. Homeward come the weary feet,
   Trudging down the village street,
   Welcomed by the sound of flute.
   Soon, oh, soon will all sounds be mute.

Now listen to this music from China
Can you hear the moon rising and setting in the music?

 High Moon ....Chinese

Phrases from
Hawaii

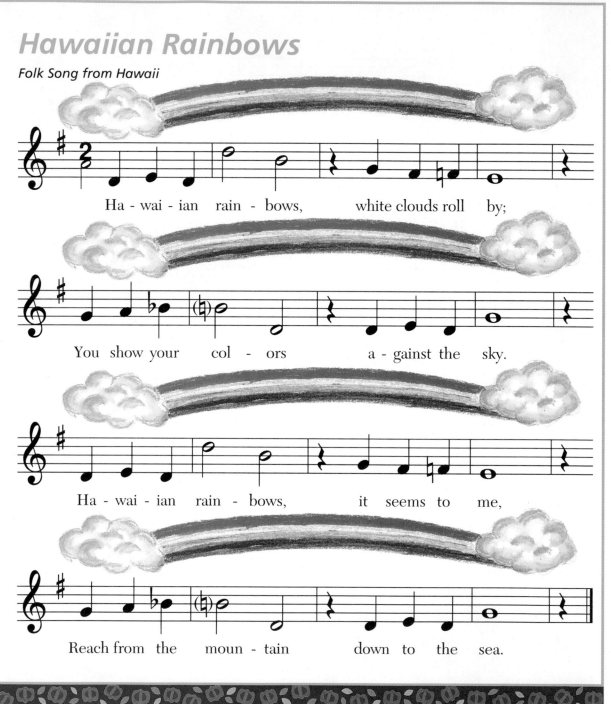

Hawaiian Rainbows

Folk Song from Hawaii

Ha - wai - ian rain - bows, white clouds roll by;

You show your col - ors a - gainst the sky.

Ha - wai - ian rain - bows, it seems to me,

Reach from the moun - tain down to the sea.

In Hawaii, dancers tell this rainbow story with their hands.

What hand motion would you use to show a rainbow?

Aquarium

Listen to this music.
Can you hear sounds that suggest beautiful, shiny fish?

"Aquarium" from *Carnival of the Animals*
...................Saint-Saëns

These fish show the shape
of the first phrase of "Aquarium."
This is how the phrase looks
in music notes.

These lines also show the shape of phrases in "Aquarium."

How are the sets of lines different from each other?

1. — _ — _ — 2. — _ — _ — _ —
   —

ABOUT THE MUSIC

Music cannot really paint pictures or tell a story. But sometimes, music helps us imagine a picture or a story. The music of "Aquarium" has a calm feeling. It helps us imagine a quiet, "fishy" world.

"Aquarium" is part of a long piece of music called *Carnival of the Animals*. It was written by the composer Camille Saint-Saëns (kah mee sa[n] sa[hn]). *Carnival of the Animals* has many sections. Each one is about a different animal.

Phrases for Baby

Willow Leaves

Willow leaves murmur, hua-la-la.
Sleep, precious baby, close to mama.
Hua-la-la, baby, smile in your sleep;
You'll have only sweet dreams
While my watch I keep.

Anonymous

Can you hear the phrases in this song?
How many are there?

Cradle Hymn

Words by Isaac Watts   *Folk Song from Kentucky*

1. Hush, my babe, lie still and slum - ber,
Ho - ly an - gels guard thy bed.
Heav'n - ly bless - ings with - out __ num - ber,
Gent - ly steal - ing __ on thy head.

2. How much better art thou tended,
Than the Son of God could be
When from heaven He descended
And became a child like thee.

3. Soft and easy is thy cradle,
Coarse and hard the Savior lay
When His birthplace was a stable
And His softest bed was hay.

From DEVIL'S DITTIES by Jean Thomas, p. 79. Copyright 1931 by W. Wilbur Hatfield. Reprinted by permission of Jean Thomas, The Traipsin' Woman.

"The Swan" from *Carnival of the Animals* ....Saint-Saëns

A Sad Story

How are the people
in these pictures alike?

How are they
different?

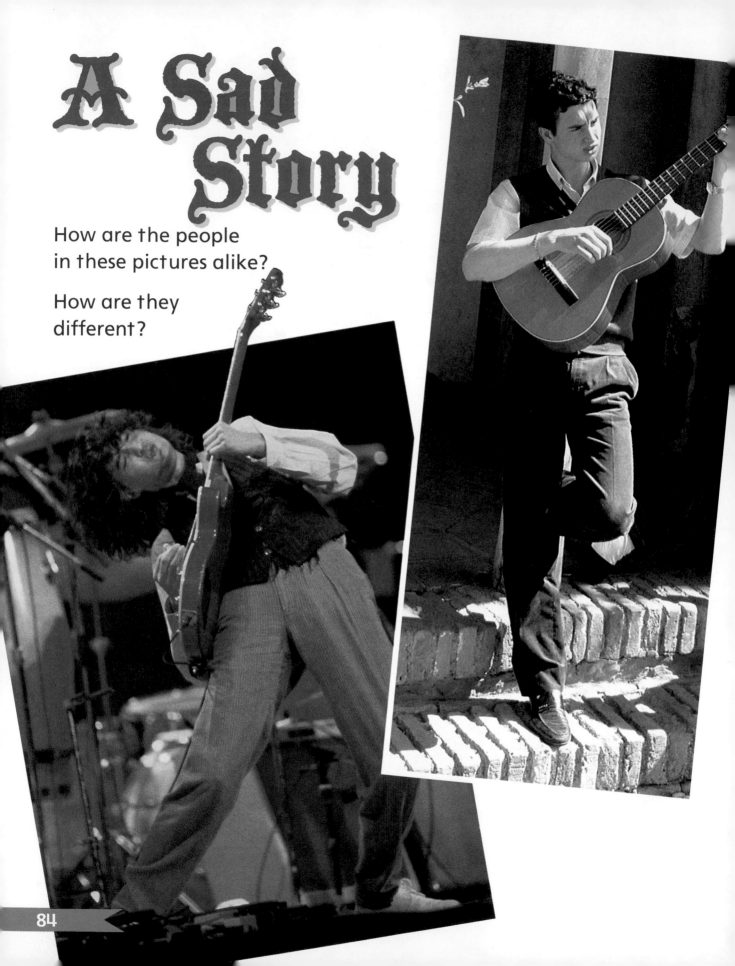

Which singer do you think would have
sung this song?

Don Alfonso

English Words by Samuel Maquí　　*Folk Song from Spain*

1.　Of　the fruit trees,　I　pre-fer　the　ros-y peach to　　oth-ers known;
2.　"In　your sad-ness, Don Al-fon - so,　may I　ask　where you are bound?"
3.　But Mer-ce - des　has de-part-ed,　she is gone, no　more to　see.

And of　the　kings of　Spain　the best　is　Don Al - fon - so　de　Bor-bón.
♪ "I　must seek my　dear　Mer-ce - des, in　Ma - drid　she can be found."
♪ She was　car-ried through the　ci - ty　by four dukes of high de-gree.

Words in Spanish

1. *De los árboles frutales*
   Me gusta el melocotón,
   Y de los reyes de España,
   Don Alfonso de Borbón.

2. *«Donde vas, Alfonso Doce?*
   Donde vas, triste de ti?»
   «Voy en busca de Mercedes
   Que hace tiempo no la vi.»

3. *Ya Mercedes está muerta,*
   Muerta está que yo la vi,
   Cuatro duques la llevaban
   Por las calles de Madrid.

Step and Leap into the Ark

Noah's Ark   *Hicks*

The animals are boarding the ark.
They look very quiet in the painting.
Do you think they were really quiet?
What do you think they sounded like?

This song tells you some of the sounds
the animals made.

Can you think of others?

Animals on Parade

Words and Music by David Eddleman

VERSES

1. Old Noah gathered in the animals,
   He led them two by two into the ark.
   He said to Missus Noah, "Look, my dear,
   We've ev'ry sort of creature from 'meow' to 'bark'!"   *Refrain*

2. It rained for forty days and forty nights,
   And covered all the earth with a heavy dew,
   But deep inside the ark old Noah thought,
   "I certainly can have my very own zoo!"   *Refrain*

REFRAIN

Meow, bark, and baa-baa, coo-coo, oink, oink, oink, what a noise they made;

Neigh - neigh   and chirp-chirp, moo-moo,   An - i - mals   on   pa - rade.

THE SUN COMES LEAPING

The Sun

Words by Louise Fabrice Hancock   Music by William S. Haynie

There's sun on the clo-ver And sun on the log,

Sun on the fish pond And sun on the frog,

Sun on the hon-ey-bee, Sun on the crows,

Sun on the wash line To dry the clean clothes.

Used by permission of Gulfport Music Company.

Look at each phrase of the song.

Which do you think is easiest to sing?

This "drawing" of each phrase
may help you decide.

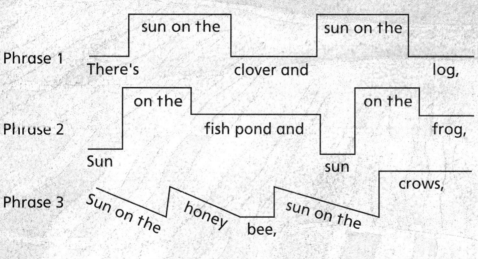

Phrase 1

```
        sun on the          sun on the
There's         clover and           log,
```

Phrase 2

```
    on the              on the
         fish pond and        frog,
Sun              sun
```

Phrase 3

```
                              crows,
Sun on the   honey      sun on the
         bee,
```

Phrase 4

Sun on the wash line to dry the clean clothes.

Listen to this song.

Does it move mostly by step or mostly by leap?

The Sun Has Got His Hat On ....Butler and Gay

PATTERNS

Find the steps, leaps and repeated tones in this song.

Chumbara

Folk Song from Québec

1. Chum - ba - ra, _____ chum - ba - ra,

Chum - ba - ra, _____ chum - ba - ra,

Chum - ba - ra, _____ chum - ba - ra,

Chum, chum, chum, chum, chum, chum, chum, chum,

Chum - ba - ra, _____ chum - ba - ra,

Chum - ba - ra, _____ chum - ba - ra,

Chum - ba - ra, _____ chum - ba - ra, Chum, chum!

2. Fy-do-lee   3. Chow-ber-ski

Shaman's Call ....Nakai

Chatter Patterns

When you chatter, you talk with someone.

Imagine talking with an angel!

Chatter with the Angels

African American Folk Song

Chat-ter with the an - gels soon in the morn - in',

Chat-ter with the an - gels in that land!

Chat-ter with the an - gels soon in the morn - in',

Chat-ter with the an - gels, join that band!

I hope to join that band

And chat-ter with the an-gels all day long!

I hope to join that band

And chat-ter with the an-gels all day long!

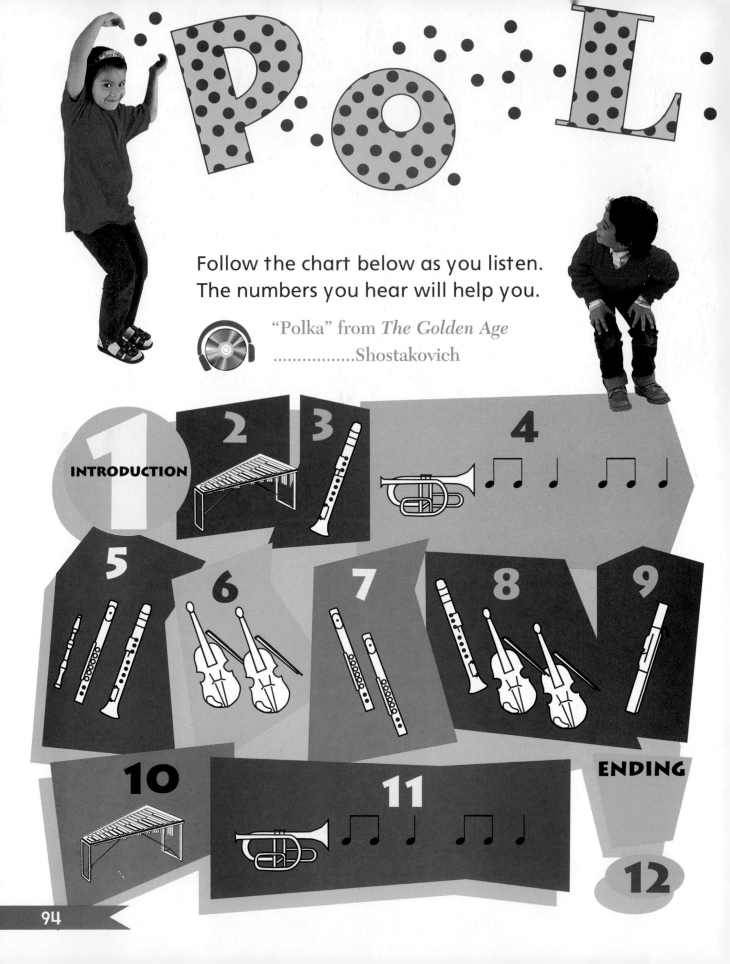

Follow the chart below as you listen.
The numbers you hear will help you.

"Polka" from *The Golden Age*
.................Shostakovich

This instrument is a trombone.

Did you hear its sliding sounds in "Polka"?
The trombone acts like a clown in this music.
It interrupts the other instruments.

Try to hear which other instruments
the trombone interrupts at number 5.

ABOUT THE MUSIC

"Polka" comes from a ballet called *The Golden Age*.
It was written by Dmitri Shostakovich (duh MEE tree
SHAH stuh KOH vitch). "Polka" is an example of a
musical joke.

The piece is full of short, happy-sounding melodies.
What a good time Shostakovich must have had writing
it. And what fun musicians have playing it!

Rooster's Repeated Rhythm

Can you find a rhythm pattern
in this song that repeats in each phrase?

Hear the Rooster Crowing
(Kum Bachur Atzel)

English Words by David ben Avraham   *Folk Song from Israel*

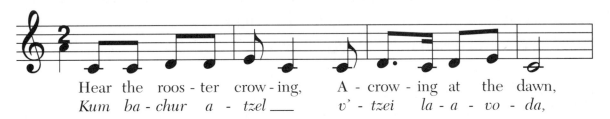

Hear the roos-ter crow-ing,   A - crow-ing at the dawn,
Kum ba-chur a - tzel ___ v' - tzei la-a-vo-da,

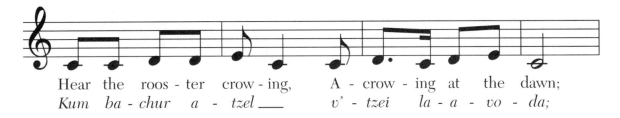

Hear the roos-ter crow-ing,   A - crow-ing at the dawn;
Kum ba-chur a - tzel ___ v' - tzei la-a-vo-da;

Wake,   wake, ___   for now   the night has gone,
Kum,   kum, ___   v' - tzei la-a-vo-da,

Wake, wake, — for now the night has gone.
Kum, kum, — v' - tzei la - u - vo - da.

Ku - ku - ri - ku, ku - ku - ri - ku, yawn a might - y yawn;
Ku - ku - ri - ku, ku - ku - ri - ku, tar n' - gol ka - ra;

Ku - ku - ri - ku, ku - ku - ri - ku, yawn a might - y yawn.
Ku - ku - ri - ku, ku - ku - ri - ku, tar n' - gol ka - ra.

Dish Rag .... Watson

Quiet Patterns in the Snow

Listen to this song.

Do you hear any rhythm patterns that repeat?

Rabbit Footprints

Words and Music by David Eddleman

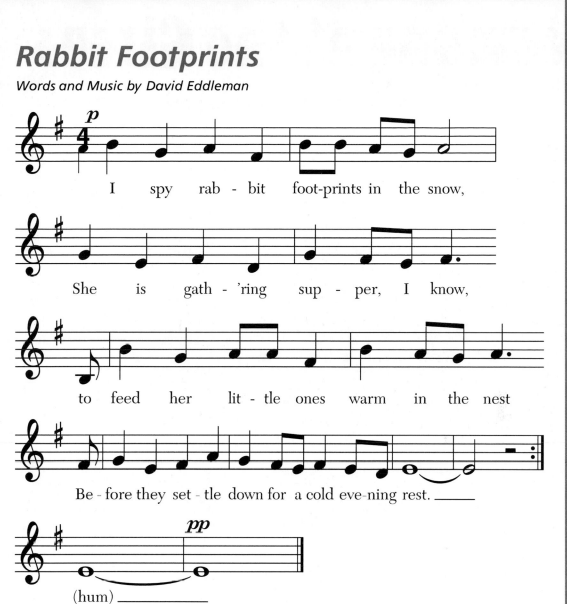

I spy rab-bit foot-prints in the snow,

She is gath-'ring sup-per, I know,

to feed her lit-tle ones warm in the nest

Be-fore they set-tle down for a cold eve-ning rest. _____

(hum) _____

When you listened to the recording, did you hear anything at the end that repeated?

Play this part on bells or metallophone at the end of the song.

Play 3 times

Harmony at the Circus

Here comes the circus band, leading the parade.

Circus Parade

Words and Music by Milton Kaye

1. Oh, here comes the cir-cus band, Ta - ra - ra - ra, ta - ra - ra - ra-ra,

Here comes the cir - cus band, Ta - ra - ra - ra - ra - ra!

REFRAIN

Zing! Zing! _____ Zing! Zing! _____

Ta - ra - ra - ra,   Ta - ra - ra - ra.

Oh, how much I love the cir - cus, Ta - ra - ra!   Boom! Boom!

2. Oh, here come the elephants,
   Clump-clump-ta-ra, clump-clump-ta-ra-ra,
   Here come the elephants,
   Clump-clump-ta-ra-ra-ra. *Refrain*

3. Oh, here come the merry clowns,
   Ha-ha-ta-ra, ha-ha-ta-ra-ra,
   Here come the merry clowns,
   Ha-ha-ta-ra-ra-ra. *Refrain*

4. Oh, here come the dancing bears,
   Thump-thump-ta-ra, thump-thump-ta-ra-ra,
   Here come the dancing bears,
   Thump-thump-ta-ra-ra-ra. *Refrain*

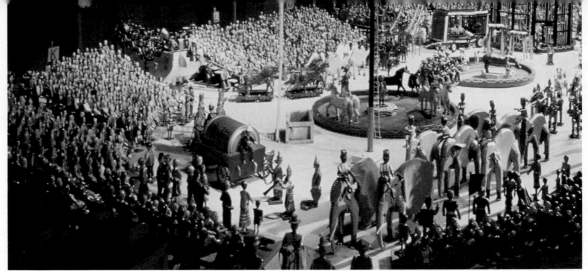

In *The Red Pony* a boy dreams about a circus.
Listen to the music that the circus band plays.

"Circus Music" from *The Red Pony*
................Copland

Bareback Riders   *W.H. Brown*

Signing in Two Styles

Sign language helps us speak to people who cannot hear.

Look at the pictures on the next page.
They show the signs for the words in this song.

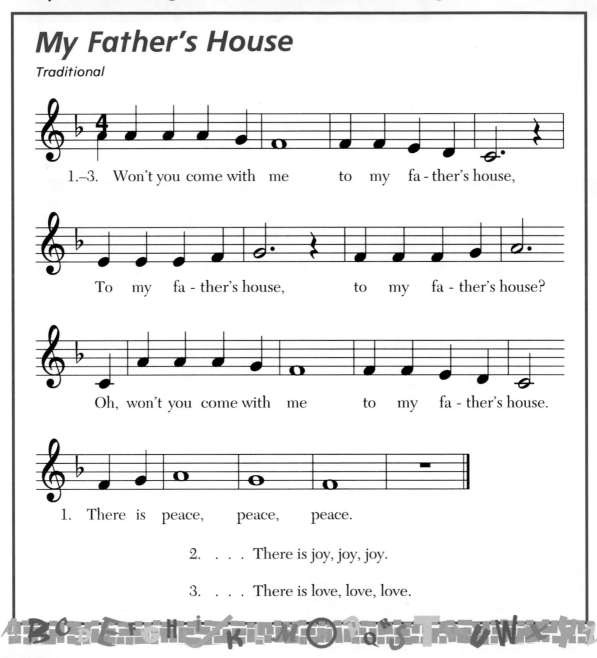

My Father's House

Traditional

1.–3. Won't you come with me to my fa - ther's house,

To my fa - ther's house, to my fa - ther's house?

Oh, won't you come with me to my fa - ther's house.

1. There is peace, peace, peace.

2. . . . There is joy, joy, joy.

3. . . . There is love, love, love.

Try to "sign" the song as you sing.

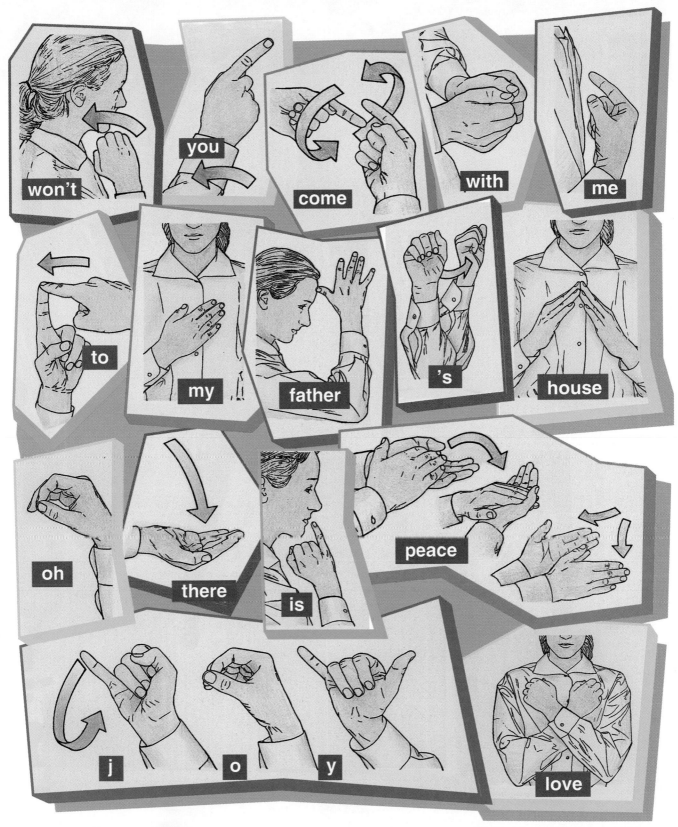

won't · you · come · with · me · to · my · father · 's · house · oh · there · is · peace · j · o · y · love

 My Father's House (gospel style) ....Traditional

Gettin' the
BLUES

You can add harmony as you sing this song.

Play these chords on autoharp as others sing.

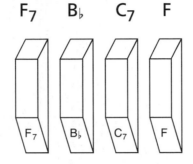

F₇   B♭   C₇   F

Good Mornin', Blues

New Words and New Musical Arrangement by Huddie Ledbetter
Edited with New Additional Material by Alan Lomax

1. Good morn - in', blues, Blues, how do you do?
2. Called yes - ter - day, Here you come to - day,

Good morn - in', blues, Blues, how do you do?
Called yes - ter - day, Here you come to - day.

I'm do - in' all right, _____ Good morn - in, how are you?
Your mouth's wide o - pen but you don't know what to say.

Putting It All Together

Sing this song
with as much feeling
as you can.

When can you sing
soft? Loud? Fast?
Slow?

Falling Rain

Words by Susan Marcus   Music by April Kassirer

REFRAIN

I can hear the fall - ing rain,

Think I'm gon - na stay in - side to - day,

Think I'm gon - na stay in - side and play

(last time to Coda)

and lis - ten to the fall - ing rain.

1. Drip, drop, drip, drop,
   Well, I'll pile my pillows way up high,
   And make a rocket ship for me to fly,
   And you can come, there's room for three,
   And we'll be back for tea. *Refrain*

2. Drip, drop, drip, drop,
   A box will be my T.V. screen,
   I'll be a monster with my face all green,
   And in a monster voice you'll hear me say,
   "Buy monster's soup today." *Refrain*

3. Drip, drop, drip, drop,
   I'll fill a fountain to the brim,
   And when it's full I'll climb right in,
   I'll keep my clothes on just in case
   I have to go someplace. *Refrain and Coda*

CODA

Drip, drop, drip, drop, And lis-ten to the fall - ing rain.

THEMES

People in our country come from many places.
Some come from Africa.
Some come from Europe.
Some come from Asia and some
from Latin America.

Some have been here
for thousands of years.
Where did your ancestors come from?

Different people have different kinds of music.
They all use music in different ways—
to express friendship, joy, sadness,
and other feelings.

The second section of your book will help you
learn how music tells us who we are.

We can understand others better
if we understand their music.

section 2

I'm Special!!

It's something to shout about!
It's great to be nobody else but me!

It's Me!

Words and Music by Carmino Ravosa

REFRAIN

It's me!   No-bod - y else but me!

(to verses)

It's me!   There's no one I'd rath - er be.

VERSES`

1. Long or short or thin or fat,
   oh, what do I care,
   When I look in the mirror just so
   long as I'm there? *Refrain*

2. Smart or dumb or weak or tough,
   there's nothing to fear
   As long as when I call myself
   I answer "Here!" *Refrain*

3. Black or white, I don't care 'bout
   the color of my skin
   As long as I've got sump'n to keep
   my insides in. *Last Refrain*

LAST REFRAIN

It's me! No-bod-y else but me!

It's me! There's no one I'd rath-er be.

It's me, it's me, it's me, it's me, it's me!

Sing!

Your mouth and voice can make different kinds of sounds.

Use your mouth and voice all three ways in this song.

Whistle While You Work

Words and Music by Larry Morey and Frank Churchill

Just whis-tle while you work. *(Whistle)* _____

Put on that grin and start right in to whis-tle loud and long.

Just hum a mer-ry tune. *(Hum)* _____

Just do your best, then take a rest and sing your-self a song.

Hum!

Whistle!

When there's too much to do, Don't let it both-er you.

For - get your trou - ble, try to be

Just like the cheer - ful chick - a - dee,

And whis - tle while you work. (Whistle) _____

Come on, get smart, tune up and start to whis - tle while you work.

Let's Go to School

Some children do a "step it down" dance to this song.

Way Down Yonder in the Schoolyard

New words and musical arrangement by Sharon, Lois and Bram   Traditional

REFRAIN

1. Way   down   yon - der   in   the   school - yard,

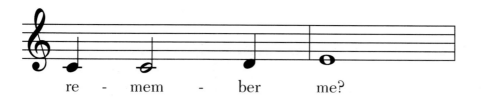

re - mem - ber   me?

Way   down   yon - der   in   the   school - yard,

re - mem - ber   me?

Well step it, step it, step it ___ down, -

re - mem - ber me? ___

You got - ta step it, step it, step it ___ down, -

Repeat 2 times

re - mem - ber me.

2. Now twirl your lover, twirl him (her) now,
   Remember me? *(2 times)*

3. Now find another, find him (her) now,
   Remember me? *(2 times)*

"Morning Mood"
from *Peer Gynt*
...........Grieg

Have you ever watched the snow fall?
Sometimes it changes as it falls.
Sometimes it drops like a heavy curtain.
Sometimes the snow swirls.
Sometimes the flakes seem to dance.

The Snow Is Dancing

Try to picture the dancing snow in this music.

"The Snow Is Dancing,"
from *Children's Corner Suite* ....Debussy

These lines show the shape of three melodies.
Can you hear the melodies in the music?

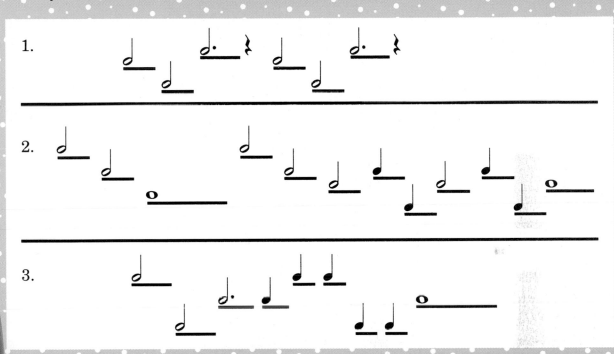

ABOUT THE MUSIC

Can you imagine a piece of music being a present?
Claude Debussy (klohd duh bew see) wrote
"The Snow Is Dancing," from *Children's Corner Suite*,
as a present for his daughter. Other pieces in the suite
are a lullaby for an elephant and a dance for a doll.

Talking with

Jon Ehrlich has been a star on Broadway. He played Huck Finn in *Big River*. Jon is also a composer.

Listen as he talks about his life as a performer and composer.

 Interview with Jon Ehrlich

Jon Ehrlich

Nobody Knows You Like I Do ......Ehrlich

Children in Mexico
use Spanish words
to count from one to ten.

Learn to count in Spanish
as you sing.

Counting Song

Words by Lucille Wood   *Children's Song from Mexico*

1. U - no, dos, y tres,   Cua - tro, cin - co, seis;

Sie - te, o - cho, nue - ve,   *I can count to* diez.

REFRAIN

La la la la la, La la la la la, La la la la la la;

La la la la la, La la la la la, La la la la la la.

2. Tengo un sombrero,

   I have a little hat;

   Tengo un sarape,

   What do you think of that? Refrain

3. Adios, amigo,

   Adios, *my friend;*

   Hasta la vista,

   Till we meet again. Refrain

A Cat that Sings

The Cat

Words by Verne Muñoz   *Folk Melody from Brazil*

1. The tom - cat has a ver - y nois - y song,

And he sings it for us all night long.

He al - ways sings the same me - ow, meow, meow,

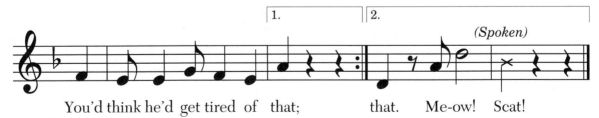

|1.| |2.| |*(Spoken)*|

You'd think he'd get tired of that;   that. Me-ow! Scat!

2. I opened up the door and chased the cat;
   Tomcat ran, that was the end of that!
   But soon I heard that old meow,
     meow, meow,   } *2 times*
   I knew that the cat was back.
   Meow! Scat!

"Love for Two Cats" from
L'Enfant et les sortilèges
............Ravel

Where is the Flower?

The Flower   (El florón)

English Words by Verne Muñoz   *Singing Game from Puerto Rico*

Pass the flow - er round and a - round.

Will it be found? Will it be found?

Where is it? Where is it? Where can the flow - er be? ____

El florón pasó por aquí,
Yo no lo vi, Yo no lo vi. } 2 times

¿Que pase, que pase,
Que pase el florón? } 2 times

A Creole song

Sing this Creole song.
Do you know who Creole people are?

Sweet Potatoes

Creole Folk Song

1. Soon as we all cook sweet po-ta-toes, Sweet po-ta-toes, Sweet po-ta-toes,

Soon as we all cook sweet po-ta-toes, Eat 'em right straight up!

2. Soon as supper's done,
   Mama hollers, . . .
   "Get along to bed!"

3. Soon's we touch our heads
   to the pillow, . . .
   Go to sleep right smart!

4. Soon's the rooster crow
   in the mornin', . . .
   Gotta wash our face!

Bamboula . . . . Gottschalk

MEET THE COMPOSER

Louis Moreau Gottschalk (1829–1869)

Louis Moreau Gottschalk (LOO ee muh ROH GOT SHAWK) was an important pianist and composer. He was one of the first truly famous American composers and performers. In his music, he used many Creole melodies.

When the Moon Is Like a Boat

In China, many songs are about the moon. In this song the moon becomes a silver boat, sailing through the sky.

Silver Moon Boat

Folk Song from China

Lit - tle sil - ver moon rides the sky like a boat,

Past the twink-ling stars it will float, light - ly float.

Sail, lit - tle moon boat, to the west,

Sail, lit - tle moon boat, while I rest.

Yeher wahn wahn shiang ee tiow troon qua tien shung,
Troon qua sheen sheen tah ee rahn cheen, ying piau dahng.
Yahng fahng shiang sho she fahng hahng.
Chiah shiao-shiao yeen troon wah ahn shung.

The Pleasure of Fishing   *Wu Wei*

ON A FARM

Can you sing the animal names in Spanish?

el burrito

My Farm

Folk Song from Argentina

1. I have a lit - tle farm be - side a wind - ing stream,

I have a lit - tle barn-yard where the grass is green.

El po - lli - to goes like this: peep, peep.

El po - lli - to goes like this: peep, peep.

el patito

el perrito

el pollito

el gatito

el chanchito

O va, ca - ma - ra - da, va, ca - ma - ra - da,

Va, o va, o va;

O va, ca - ma - ra - da, va, ca - ma - ra - da,

Va, o va, o va.

2. *El patito* goes like this: quack, quack.

3. *El burrito* goes like this: hee haw.

4. *El chanchito* goes like this: oink, oink.

5. *El perrito* goes like this: woof, woof.

6. *El gatito* goes like this: meow, meow.

Achshav!

Awake! Awake! (Achshav)

English Words by David ben Avraham   *Folk Song from Israel*

A - wake!   A - wake!   the val - leys   of   our   land,
Ach - shav,   *ach - shav,*   *b' - em - ek   Yis - ra - el;*

A - wake!   A - wake!   the val - leys   of   our   land.
Ach - shav,   *ach - shav,*   *b' - em - ek   Yis - ra - el.*

Tum - ba, tum - ba, tum - ba,   the land of   Is - ra - el,   Hey!
Tum - ba, tum - ba, tum - ba,   b' - em - ek   Yis - ra - el,   Hey!

Tum - ba, tum - ba, tum - ba,   the land of   Is - ra - el,   Hey!
Tum - ba, tum - ba, tum - ba,   b' - em - ek   Yis - ra - el,   Hey!

Achshav is a Hebrew word that means *now*.
In what country do people speak Hebrew?
Can you sing this song in both English and Hebrew?

Take Me to the World .... Ehrlich

Ev'rybody's

Listen to this song.
Sometimes a word is left out.
Sing a friend's name in place of it to welcome him or her.

Ev'rybody's Welcome

Folk Song from Tennessee

Ev - 'ry-bod - y's wel - come, _ yes, yes, wel - come!

Ev - 'ry-bod - y's wel - come, _ come a-long and go.

Oh, glo - ry, hal - le - lu - jah!

Oh, glo - ry, come a-long and go.

From *SONGS OF THE OLD CAMP GROUND,* compiled by L. L. McDowell. Reprinted by permission.

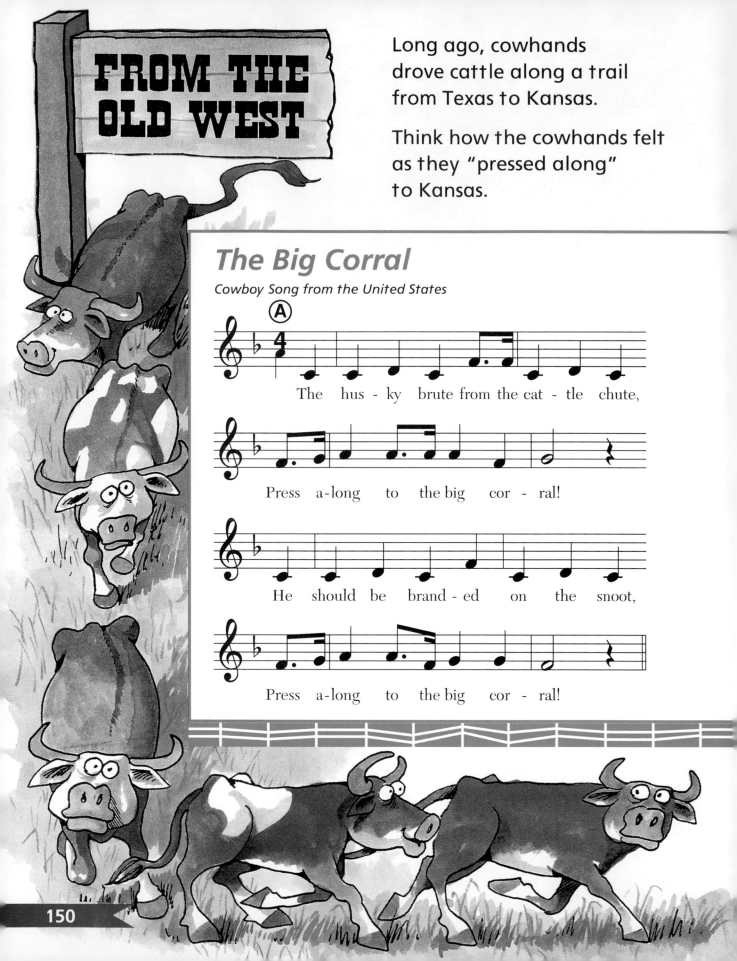

FROM THE OLD WEST

Long ago, cowhands drove cattle along a trail from Texas to Kansas.

Think how the cowhands felt as they "pressed along" to Kansas.

The Big Corral

Cowboy Song from the United States

Ⓐ

The hus-ky brute from the cat-tle chute,

Press a-long to the big cor-ral!

He should be brand-ed on the snoot,

Press a-long to the big cor-ral!

Play this bell part during section A.

Bells
Play 7 times

C D C C F

Play this pattern on wood block in Section B.

Play 4 times.

B **REFRAIN**

Press a - long, cow - boy,

Press a-long with a cow - boy yell, Ya - hoo!

Press a - long, cow - boy,

Press a-long to the big cor - ral!

TO KANSAS

the First Americans

Before there was a United States of America, there was the land. Many people lived in this land. The people belonged to different nations.

Listen to this dance from the Kiowa nation.
Men danced this dance before they went
to hunt buffalo.

Buffalo Dance Song ....Traditional Kiowa

Mothers of the Chippewa nation sang this song
to their babies.

Chippewa Lullaby

Collected by Frances Densmore, 1913

Way   o   way   o   way _____

way   o   way   o   way _____

way   o   way   o _____

The Inuit people live in Alaska and Canada.
Often they are called Eskimos.
Sometimes Inuit sing to call
for good weather.

Eskimo Weather Incantation
................Traditional

Our Wonderful Home

We are proud of our country.
We sing songs that tell of its freedom.

America

Traditional   Words by Samuel Francis Smith

1. My coun-try! 'tis of thee, Sweet land of lib-er-ty,

Of thee I sing;

Land where my fa-thers died, Land of the Pil-grims' pride,

From ev-'ry moun-tain-side Let free-dom ring!

2. Our fathers' God, to Thee,   Long may our land be bright
   Author of liberty,   With freedom's holy light;
   To Thee we sing;   Protect us by Thy might,
                                 Great God, our King!

Mount Moran, Autumn   Grand Teton National Park, Wyoming   *Ansel Adams*

Irving Berlin was a great American songwriter.
He praised our country in a famous song.
How does he describe America?

 God Bless America ....Berlin

Do you ever dream about walking on the moon? The child in this song does.

Mission Control

Words and Music by Carmino Ravosa

Mis-sion Con-trol, __ do you read me?

Will you please save __ me a place?

Mis-sion Con-trol, __ do you need me

On the next rock-et in space?

1. May-be I'm small, _ but I'm grow-ing.

Watch, and one day __ you will see.

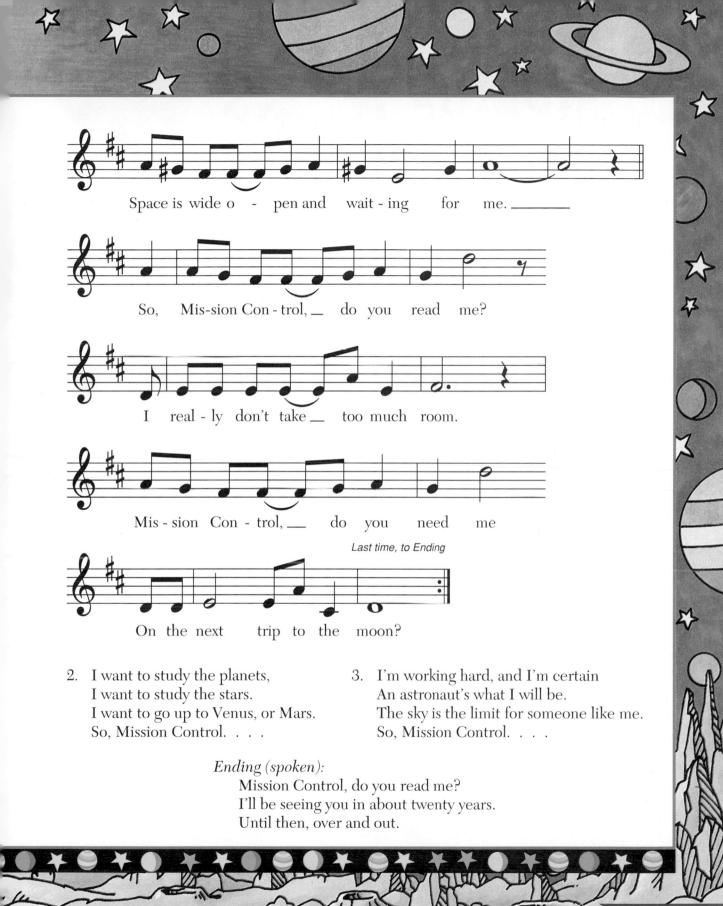

Space is wide o - pen and wait-ing for me. _____

So, Mis-sion Con-trol, _ do you read me?

I real - ly don't take _ too much room.

Mis - sion Con-trol, _ do you need me

Last time, to Ending

On the next trip to the moon?

2. I want to study the planets,
   I want to study the stars.
   I want to go up to Venus, or Mars.
   So, Mission Control. . . .

3. I'm working hard, and I'm certain
   An astronaut's what I will be.
   The sky is the limit for someone like me.
   So, Mission Control. . . .

Ending (spoken):
        Mission Control, do you read me?
        I'll be seeing you in about twenty years.
        Until then, over and out.

A Singing Game

These workers sing about their good life. They call it *la buena, buena vida*.

San Severino

Folk Song from Chile

San   Se - ve - ri - no,   la   bue - na,   bue - na   vi - da;

San   Se - ve - ri - no,   la   bue - na,   bue - na   vi - da;

Play this pattern on claves each time you hear it.

Now this way and now that

1. Now this way and now that,   so goes *el car-pin-te-ro;*

A-*sí, a-sí, a-sí,*   this is the life for me.

2. Now this way and now that, so goes *el zapatero* . . .

3. Now this way and now that, so goes *el panadero* . . .

4. Now this way and now that, so goes *el caballero* . . .

TEAMING UP

Working together gets things done.
Teamwork can be very important.

Working Together

Words and Music by Carmino Ravosa

REFRAIN

Work-ing to-geth-er, work-ing to-geth-er,

(Last time shouted)

Fine

Work-ing to-geth-er, We get things done.
Is lots more fun.

Chorus (Echo)

1. Ev - 'ry - one at home should pitch in,
2. We should, in each town and ci - ty,
3. Did you know the fin - est la - bor?

Chorus (Echo)

D.C.

From the out - side to the kit - chen,
Try to keep it clean and pret - ty,
It is when you help your neigh - bor,

The Acrobats *Demuth*

Listen to Carmino Ravosa talk about his life in music.

Interview with Carmino Ravosa

© 1919. Water color and pencil on paper, 13 x 7/8." The Museum of Modern Art, New York. Gift of Abby Aldrich Rockefeller.

The American Indian Dance Theater

American Indians
are well known
for their exciting dances.

American Indians
from several nations
formed a company
to perform their songs
and dances.

Listen as they talk
about American Indian life.

*Interview
with Members
of the American Indian
Dance Theater*

A Ribbon Dance from China

People in China do a lovely dance with ribbons.
Listen to the music.

Try playing the melody on bells
or some other mallet instrument.

Ribbon Dance

Folk Dance from China

From Edna Doll and Mary Jarman Nelson, *Rhythms Today!* © 1965 by the Silver Burdett Company.

You can play these parts to accompany the music.

Finger Cymbals

Temple Blocks

Gong (last measure only)

Making Your Own Music

Find a glockenspiel or xylophone
and arrange the bars like this.

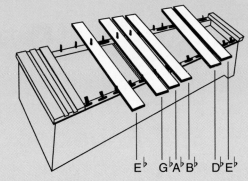

Make up a part to go with the music.

Use a rhythm from words you make up, such as
"How I love to play along," or "Dancing is a lot of fun."

Play any bar you wish.
Try different patterns.

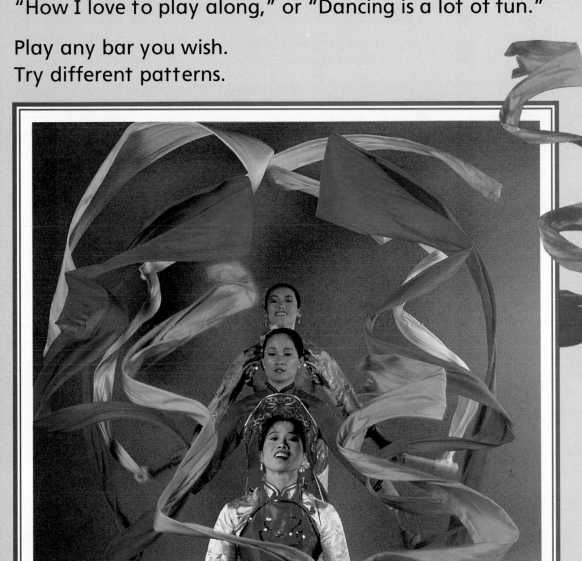

BOUNCING BALLS

In Japan, children sing about bouncing balls. Imagine bouncing a ball on each beat.

Ball-Bouncing Song (Maritsuki-uta)

Children's Song from Japan

Ten, ten, ten, I bought a lit-tle ball while at the fair.
Ten, ten, ten, Ten-jin sa-ma-no o-mat-su-ni de,

Ten, ten, ten cents was the price that I paid there.
Ten, ten te-ma-ri o ka-i-ma-shi-ta.

Ten, ten, where then shall I bounce my lit-tle ball?
Ten ten, te-ma-ri wa do-ko de tsu-ku,

There 'neath the plum tree that is stand-ing straight and tall,
U-me no o-ha-na no shi-ta de tsu-ka,

stand-ing straight and tall.
shi-ta de tsu-ka.

From THE MELODY BOOK by Patricia Hackett. Used by permisson of Prentice-Hall.

An African Dance

In Ghana, children play a follow-the-leader game with this song.

Learn to sing the song, then try the game. Can you hear the follow-the-leader parts in the song?

Che Che Koolay

Folk Song from Ghana

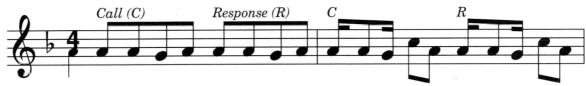

Che-che koo-lay, Che-che koo-lay, Che-che ko-fee sa, Che-che ko-fee sa,

Ko-fee sa-lan-ga, Ko-fee sa-lan-ga. Ka-ka-shee lan-ga, Ka-ka-shee lan-ga.

Whoops! Ah lye lye! Whoops! Ah lye lye!

Ronde and Saltarello

This music is dance music.
Listen to the recording.

Do you think the dance
was like the ones we do today?

Ronde.................Susato

Palazzo Pubblico, Siena. Scandia/Art Resource, NY

The Effect of Good Government in the City (detail) *Lorenzetti*

Now listen to the same music played a different way.

 Saltarello ....*Susato*

ABOUT THE MUSIC

Ronde and *Saltarello* are dance pieces written in the 1500s by Tielman Susato (TEEL muhn soo ZAH toh). Susato wanted them played on any instruments that people had. You have heard the dances played on brass instruments. How do you think they would sound on flutes? Or on violins? Or on guitar? *Ronde* and *Saltarello* have the same melody, but they use it in different ways.

There She Blows!

Once upon a time there were many whales
in the ocean. Now there are only a few.
People have hunted them down, and they are rare.
Dolphins and seals, too, are in danger.

Can you imagine a world with no whales, dolphins, or seals?

A Whale of a Tale

Words and Music by Gene Grier and Lowell Everson

REFRAIN

We've a whale of a tale to share with you,

a whale of a tale you see, ___ a - bout our friends who live with us

to verses

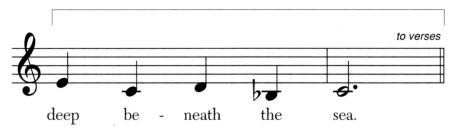

deep be - neath the sea.

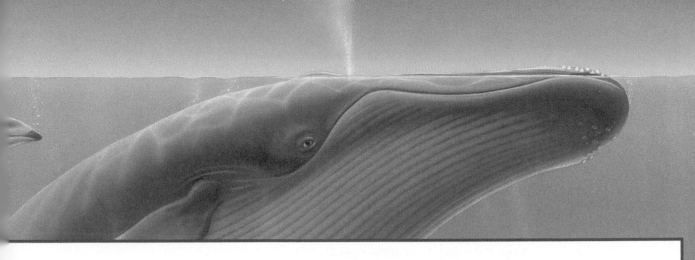

VERSES

1. Now, Mister Whale, he has a tail
   as big as it can be,
   And when it flips, he dives below,
   deep beneath the sea.

2. Now, Missus Seal has flippers, too,
   as cute as they can be,
   And when they flip, she dives below,
   deep beneath the sea.

3. Now, Mister Dolphin, he's so smart,
   as smart as he can be,
   And fish the smartest fish we know,
   deep beneath the sea.

4. Now, dolphins, seals and whales, my friends,
   endangered are all three,
   And it's up to us to save them all,
   deep beneath the sea.   *Refrain*

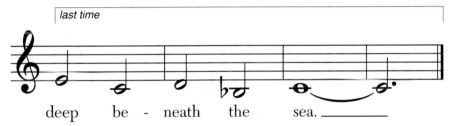

last time

deep   be - neath   the   sea. _____

Whales talk to each other with clicks and whistles.
Listen to the whales singing in this piece.

Whales Alive (excerpt)
................Winter

Recycling Center

Recycle Rap

Words and Music by Gene Grier and Lowell Everson

(Spoken in a rap style)

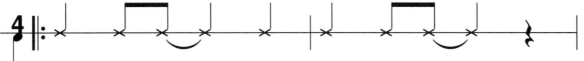

1. Pa - per, cans ___ and e - ven glass ___
2. When you shop, ___ re - mem - ber this, ___
3. Pa - per can ___ be used a - gain. ___

real - ly make ___ some nas - ty trash. ___
plas - tics make ___ some nas - ty trash. ___
Save those bot - tles, turn them in. ____

It is a waste to throw away things that can be
used again.
Paper, glass, and cans can be used over and over.

This rap tells you about recycling.

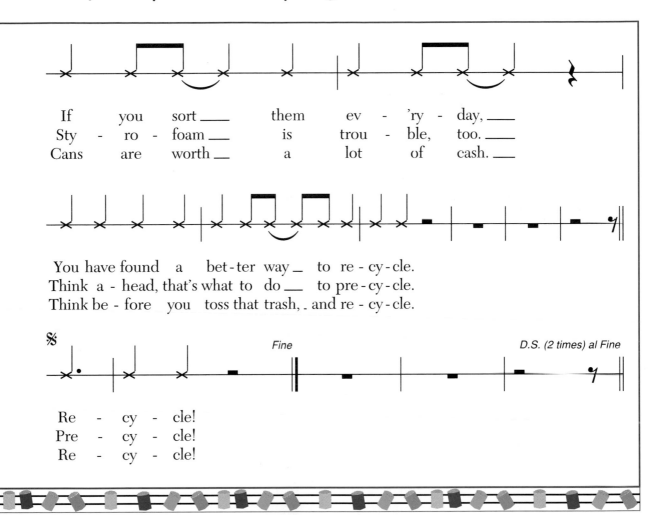

If   you   sort ___   them   ev - 'ry - day, ___
Sty - ro - foam ___   is   trou - ble,   too. ___
Cans   are   worth ___   a   lot   of   cash. ___

You have found   a   bet-ter way _ to re - cy - cle.
Think a - head, that's what to do __ to pre-cy - cle.
Think be - fore   you   toss that trash, _ and re - cy - cle.

Fine   *D.S. (2 times) al Fine*

Re   -   cy - cle!
Pre -   cy - cle!
Re   -   cy - cle!

Keeping the Ocean Healthy

So many creatures live in the ocean.

From Sea to Shining Sea

Words and Music by Gene Grier and Lowell Everson

Solo

1. Oil and wa - ter, they just don't mix;
2. Su - per tank - er crashed on a reef;
3. Oil and wa - ter, they just don't mix;

that's a guar - an - tee.
was - n't meant __ to be.
that's a guar - an - tee.

Fish and wild - life get ver - y sick
Beach - es cov - ered with oil and grease
Fish and wild - life get ver - y sick

3rd time to Coda ⊕

from sea to shin - ing sea.
from sea to shin - ing sea.
from sea to shin - ing sea.

We can all help
to keep the water
clean for them.

Chorus

From sea to shin - ing sea,

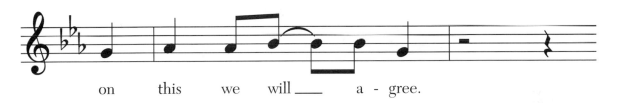

on this we will ___ a - gree.

To keep the wa - ter free

from ref - use and ___ de - bris.

Coda

From sea to shin - ing sea, from sea to shin - ing sea.

Let It Rain

It's Raining, It's Raining (Que llueva)

English Words by Samuel Maquí   Game Song from Mexico

It's rain - ing, it's rain - ng,
Que llue - va, que llue - va,

The frog is in his cot - tage,
La ra - na es - tá en la cue - va,

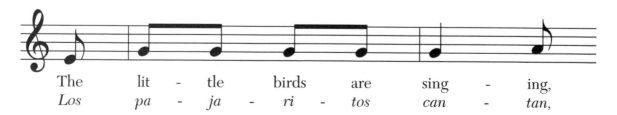

The lit - tle birds are sing - ing,
Los pa - ja - ri - tos can - tan,

Rain helps us in many ways.
We need clean rain.

This song tells about the rain
and how happy it makes everyone.

Children in Mexico play
a game with this song. The game
is a way to say "thank you" for the rain.

The sil - ver moon is ris - ing,
La lu - na se le - van - ta,

Yes, yes,
Que sí,

1.

no, no! The fall - ing rain is here.
que no! Que cai - ga un cha - pa - rron.

2.

no, no! The far - mer hears it sing.
que no! Le can - ta el la - bra - dor.

Spooky Sounds

What things does this song tell you about the witch?
What sounds will you choose to describe her?

There Once Was a Witch

Traditional

1. There once was a witch, Be-lieve it if you can,

She tapped on the win-dows and she ran, ran,— ran.

She ran hel-ter-skel-ter with her toes in the air,

Corn-stalks fly-ing from the witch-'s hair!

2. "Swish," goes the broomstick.
   "Meow," goes the cat.
   "Plop," goes the hoptoad
   sitting on her hat.

   "Whee!" chuckled I,
   "What fun! What fun!"
   Halloween night when the
   witches run.

Henry Cowell played the inside of the piano
to get the sounds in *The Banshee*.

 The Banshee ....Cowell

Halloween Is a Very Unusual Night

Words and Music by Ned Ginsburg

1. There's only one night like this all year,
   Only one night when spirits appear;
   An evening meant to be spent outside,
   Yes, it's Halloween, and you cannot hide.

2. Drop your fears and off you go,
   join the traveling costume show.
   Grab your sack and attack the street,
   But you better start to trick-or-treat.

REFRAIN

When the ghosts come out,

and the gob - lins creep,

and the skel - e - tons rat - tle.

How could an - y - bod - y sleep?

And the mon - sters march,

while the witch - es take flight.

D.C. (verse 2)
last time to

Yes, Hal - lo - ween is a ver - y un - u - su - al night!

Coda

Yes, Hal - lo - ween is a ver - y un - u - su - al night!

A Holiday

Over the River and Through the Wood

Words by Lydia Maria Child   *Traditional*

1. O - ver the riv - er and through the wood,

To Grand - fa - ther's house we go; _____

The horse knows the way to car - ry the sleigh

Thro' the white and drif - ted snow. _____

Visit

O - ver the riv - er and through the wood,

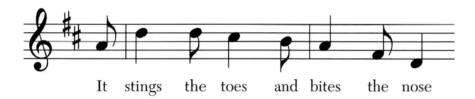

Oh, how the wind does blow! ____

It stings the toes and bites the nose

As o - ver the ground we go.

2. Over the river and through the wood,
   Trot fast, my dapple gray!
   Spring over the ground like a
      hunting hound,
   For this is Thanksgiving Day!

Over the river and through the wood,
Now Grandmother's face I spy!
Hurrah for the fun! Is the
   pudding done?
Hurrah for the pumpkin pie!

A Musical Sleigh Ride
............L. Mozart

Being Thankful

In November we set aside a day for giving thanks.

Thanksgiving

English Words by Rosemary Jacques *Folk Tune from Finland*

1. For the sun that gives us light,

We are tru - ly thank - ful.

For the moon that shines at night,

We are tru - ly thank - ful.

Oil on canvas, 1935, 71.4 x 101.6 cm, Mr. and Mrs. Frank G. Logan Prize Fund, 1935.313. The Art Institute of Chicago. All Rights Reserved.

Thanksgiving   Doris Lee (American, 1905-1982)

For the twink-ling stars so ___ bright,

We are tru - ly thank - ful.

2. For the corn and golden wheat,
    We are truly thankful.
    For the pears and apples sweet, . . .
    For the good food that we eat, . . .

3. For the joys of each new day, . . .
    For each hour of work and play, . . .
    For God's blessings, let us say,
    "We are truly thankful."

A Celebration

Candles are lighted for Chanukah.
How many are lighted on the first night?
On the last night?

In the Window

English Words by Judith K. Eisenstein   *Jewish Folk Melody*

1. In the win - dow, where you can send your glow

From my me - no - rah on new - ly fall - en snow,

I will set you one lit - tle can - dle

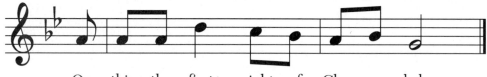

On this the first night of Cha - nu - kah.

2. In the window, where you can send your glow
   From my menorah on newly fallen snow,
   I will set you two little candles
   On this the second night of Chanukah.

3. . . . three . . . third . . .
4. . . . four . . . fourth . . .
5. . . . five . . . fifth . . .

6. . . . six . . . sixth . . .
7. . . . seven . . . seventh . . .
8. . . . eight . . . eighth . . .

from THE GATEWAY TO JEWISH SONG by Judith Eisenstein. Reprinted by permission of the author.

Spin the Dreydl

Children sing songs and play games to celebrate Chanukah.
This song tells about the dreydl game.

Joyous Chanukah

English Words by Phyllis Resnick   Hebrew Folk Song

Cha - nu - kah,   Cha - nu - kah,   hol - i - day   so   fair,

Glow - ing   light,   can - dles   bright,   hap - pi - ness   we   share.

Gai - ly   dance,   gai - ly   sing   while   the   drey - dl   whirls,

Round and   round,   round and   round,   see   how   fast   it   twirls.

Here is a part to play on the tambourine.

Play 4 times

Shake

Fantasy for Chanukah ....ben Avraham

A SLEIGH RIDE

Have you ever been on a sleigh ride?
Imagine what it would be like?

Jingle Bells

Words and Music by James Pierpont

Dashing through the snow, in a one-horse open sleigh,
O'er the fields we go, laughing all the way.
Bells on Bobtail ring, making spirits bright;
What fun it is to ride and sing a sleighing song tonight!

REFRAIN

Jin - gle bells, jin - gle bells, Jin - gle all the way!

Oh, what fun it is to ride

In a one-horse o - pen sleigh! —

Jin - gle bells, jin - gle bells, Jin - gle all the way!

Oh, what fun it is to ride

In a one - horse o - pen sleigh!

A One-Way Conversation

Can you find another name for Saint Nicholas in this song?

Jolly Old Saint Nicholas

Traditional

B   A   G

1. Jol - ly old Saint Ni - cho - las, Lean your ear this way,

Don't you tell a sin - gle soul What I'm going to say;

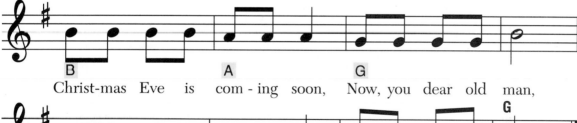

B   A   G

Christ-mas Eve is com - ing soon, Now, you dear old man,

G

Whis - per what you'll bring to me, Tell me if you can.

2. When the clock is striking twelve,
   When I'm fast asleep,
   Down the chimney tall and round,
   With your pack you'll creep;
   All the stockings you will find
   Hanging in a row;
   Mine will be the shortest one,
   You'll be sure to know.

3. Johnny wants a pair of skates,
   Susie wants a toy,
   Nancy wants a storybook,
   One to bring her joy;
   As for me, I'm not too sure,
   So I'll say "goodnight,"
   Choose for me, dear Santa Claus,
   What you think is right.

Presents Pouring Down

Children in Mexico break open a piñata to get presents.

La piñata

English Words by Louis C. Adelman   *Folk Song from Mexico*   *Collected by Natividad Vacio*

1. When po - sa - das days are here a - gain, The pi - ña - ta has a spe - cial place.

All the boys and girls, though well-be-haved, Have a mer-ry, mer-ry chase!

REFRAIN

See the gay pi - ña - ta, hang-ing high a - bove you,
Break the gay pi - ña - ta, send the can - dy fly - ing,

Swing un - til you find it, swing and break it o - pen!
Fill up all the bas - kets with all kinds of good - ies.

2. With a blindfold 'round your shining eyes, The piñata breaks in pieces
   With a big stick in your swinging hand, And the treats we meet are grand.

Refrain

190

A Famous Carol

"Silent Night" was written
because a church organ broke down.

It is one of the world's best-loved carols.

Silent Night

Words by Joseph Mohr   Music by Franz Gruber

Si - lent night, ho - ly night,

All   is   calm,   all   is   bright

Round yon vir - gin moth - er and child.

Ho - ly in - fant so ten - der and mild,

Sleep   in heav - en - ly   peace, ___

Sleep __ in heav - en - ly   peace. ___

A Celebration

Children in Spain sing this song.

Zumba, zumba

English Words by Margaret Marks   *Folk Song from Spain*

REFRAIN

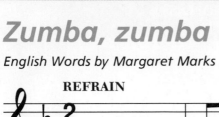

¡Zum - ba, zum - ba! Strike the cym - bal.

¡Zum - ba, zum - ba! Strike the gong.

¡Zum - ba, zum - ba! Beat the tim - bal

Fine

And the tam - bou - rine and drum!

VERSES

1. Born on this night is a baby.
   Ev'ryone brings him a present,
   Brings him a savory meat-pie
   Made out of partridge and pheasant.
   Refrain

2. What shall I take to the baby?
   What shall I say when I take it?
   I'll bring a gourd for a rattle,
   I'll ask his mother to shake it.
   Refrain

The Eve of Saint Nicholas   Jan Steen

A Freedom Song

Free at Last

African American Spiritual

Free at last, __ free at last, __

Thank God Al - might - y, I'm free at last, __

Free at last, __ free at last, _____

Fine

Thank God Al - might - y, I'm free at last. __

1. 'Way down yonder in the graveyard walk,
   Thank God Almighty, I'm free at last.
   Me and my Jesus gonna meet and talk,
   Thank God Almighty, I'm free at last.

2. On a my knees when the light passed by,
   Thank God Almighty, I'm free at last.
   Thought my soul would rise and fly,
   Thank God Almighty, I'm free at last.

3. Some of these mornings, bright and fair,
   Thank God Almighty, I'm free at last.
   Gonna meet King Jesus in the air,
   Thank God Almighty, I'm free at last.

A Cry for Freedom

Harriet Tubman

Black Heritage USA 13¢

Oh, Freedom

African American Spiritual

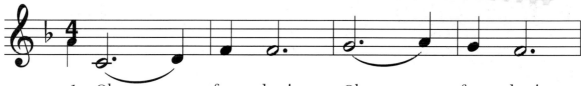

1. Oh, _____ free - dom! Oh, _____ free - dom!
2. No more cry - in', no more cry - in',
3. There'll be sing - in', there'll be sing - in',
4. Oh, _____ free - dom! Oh, _____ free - dom!

Oh, _____ free - dom o - ver me. _____
No more cry - in', o - ver me! _____
There'll be sing - in', o - ver me! _____
Oh, _____ free - dom, o - ver me! _____

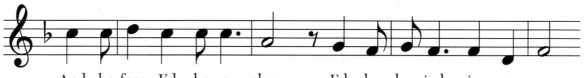

And be - fore I'd be a slave, I'd be bur - ied in my grave,

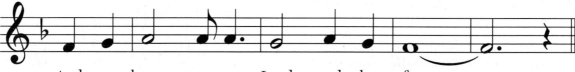

And go home to my Lord and be free.

The New Year Dragons Are Coming

At Chinese New Year there are fireworks and parades.
Dragons wind through the streets.
People dance and sing to welcome New Year.

Chinese New Year

Words and Music by Low Siew Poh

1. Chi - nese New Year is here a - gain,

Here a - gain, here a - gain,

Chi - nese New Year is here a - gain,

Let us all re - joice. _____

2. Look at the dragon breathing flames,
   Breathing flames, breathing flames,
   Look at the dragon breathing flames,
   Roar, roar, roar.

3. Dragon is leaping with the drum, . . .
   Leap, leap, leap.

4. Children have packets of money to spend,
   Clink, clink, clink.

5. Everyone dances through the streets, . . .
   Let us all rejoice.

196

A Valentine for You

What makes this such a good Valentine song? Is it the music? Is it the words? Find a partner and walk to the steady beat.

Valentine

Words and Music by April Kassirer

REFRAIN

Won't you be my val - en - tine? ___

Won't you be a friend of mine? ___

It would make me feel so fine ___

If you'd be my val - en - tine.

1. Maybe we could walk together.
   Walking is a very enjoyable way
   For two or more to spend time together.
   "Look at all the fun they're having."
   That's what everyone would say, so, *Refrain*

2. Maybe we could talk together.
   Talking is a very enjoyable way. . . *Refrain*

Waltz on the Ice ....Prokofiev

An Old Favorite

The original painting hangs in the Selectmen's Meeting Room, Abbot Hall, Marblehead, Ma.

The Spirit of '76   *Archibald M. Willard (1836-1918)*

Do you think the musicians in the picture are playing "Yankee Doodle"?

What other songs about our country do you know?

Yankee Doodle

Words by Dr. Richard Shuckburgh   Traditional

1. Fath'r and I went down to camp,
A - long with Cap - tain Good - in',
And there we saw the men and boys
As thick as hast - y pud - din'.

REFRAIN

Yan - kee Doo - dle, keep it up, Yan - kee Doo - dle dan - dy,

Mind the mu - sic and the step And with the girls be hand - y.

2. And there was Captain Washington
   Upon a slappin' stallion,
   A-giving orders to his men;
   I guess there was a million. *Refrain*

A MEXICAN HAPPY BIRTHDAY

How is this song different
from "Happy Birthday to You"?

Las mañanitas

English Version by Lupe Allegria   *Folk Song from Mexico*

Hear us sing *las ma - ña - ni - tas,* as the morn-ing light ap-pears,
Es - tas son las ma - ña - ni - tas, Que can - ta - ba el Rey Da - vid,

And the gen - tle bird will join in the hap-py mu - sic he hears.
A las mu - cha-chas bo - ni - tas Se las can - ta - mos a - quí.

Oh, wake up and see the sun-shine. Oh, wake up and meet the day.
Des - pier - ta, mi bien, des - pier - ta, Mi - ra que ya a - ma - ne - ció;

Hear, the morn-ing bird is sing-ing, the sil-ver moon has gone a - way.
Ya los pa - ja - ri - llos can-tan, La lu - na ya ___ se me - tió.

A Song to America

America, I Hear You Singing

Words and Music by Barberi Paull

A - mer - i - ca, I hear you sing-ing,
When I sing _ out your joy - ous an-them,

A - mer - i - ca, your old sweet song;
Yes, ev - 'ry _ time of you I sing,

Our dreams and _ hopes, it seems, are borne,
I join your _ song, A - mer - i - ca,

A - mer - i - ca, in your song. _____
I join in your free - dom song. _____

Ev'rybody Smiles in

A Theme Musical

the Same Language

by Carmino Ravosa

Ev'rybody Smiles in the Same Language

Words and Music by Carmino Ravosa

Solo (1st time), Chorus (2nd time)
Swing style

You're a Friend of Mine

Words and Music by Carmino Ravosa

Solos (1st and 2nd times)
Chorus (3rd time)

1., 2. You're a   friend of   mine,   You're a   friend of   mine;
3. You're a   friend of   mine,   You're a   friend of   mine;

But   I don't want to play with you though you're a friend of mine.
And, yes, I   want to play with you, 'cause you're a friend of mine.

You're a   friend of   mine,   You're a   friend of   mine;
You're a   friend of   mine,   You're a   friend of   mine;

Fine

But   I don't want to play with you though you're a friend of mine.
And, yes, I   want to play with you, 'cause you're a friend of mine.

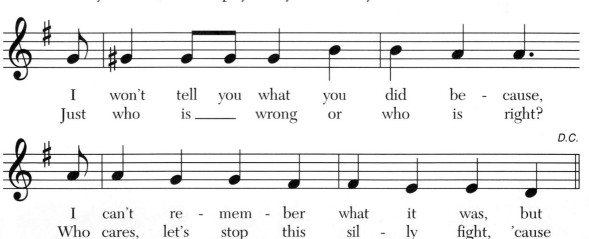

I   won't   tell   you   what   you   did   be - cause,
Just   who   is _____   wrong   or   who   is   right?

D.C.

I   can't   re - mem - ber   what   it   was,   but
Who cares,   let's   stop   this   sil - ly   fight, 'cause

People

Words by Charlotte Zolotow   Music by Carmino Ravosa

Solo (1st time), Chorus (2nd time)

Some peo - ple talk and talk and nev - er say a thing.

Some peo - ple look at you, and birds be - gin to sing.

Some peo - ple laugh and laugh, and yet you want to cry,

rit (2nd time)   *Fine*

Some peo-ple touch your hand, and mu - sic fills the sky.

D.C. al Fine

Why it hap-pens, why it's so, I can't ex-plain it, but this I know.

What's a Teacher to Do?

Words and Music by Carmino Ravosa

Solo (1st time), Chorus (other times)

What's a teach - er to do?

Hav - ing chil - dren like you.

What's a teach - er to, what's a teach - er to,

What's a teach - er to do?

Solo (all verses)

D.C. al (last time)

1. How man - y times must I say, This is not the time to play?
2. You'll have __ some kids tug-ging you. And some oth-ers hug-ging you.
3. But by the end of ev - 'ry day, You kids steal my heart a - way.

Coda

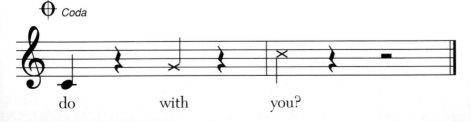

do with you?

We Speak the Same Language

Words and Music by Carmino Ravosa

We speak the same lan - guage, me and __ you. __
yes, we __ do. __

Fine

We speak the same lan - guage, me and __ you, __ we do. __

It is the thing __ that __ kept __ us __ to-geth - er,
It is the thing __ that __ holds __ us __ to-geth - er, The

Kept us from fall - ing a - part.
rea - son that we've __ come so far.

It is the thing __ that __ kept __ us __ to-geth - er,
It is the thing __ that __ holds __ us __ to-geth - er,

D.C. (al Fine after last verse)

From the ver - y start.
Made us what we are.

A Little Bit More of Love

Words and Music by Carmino Ravosa

Solo (1st time), Chorus (2nd and 3rd times)

What we need in this world is ____

a lit - tle bit more of ____ love. ____

To ⊕ 3rd time

A lit - tle bit more of, ___ a lit - tle bit more of ___ love. _

You can be hap - py, You can be hap - py, On - ly if you do __

rit. (3rd time) *D.C. (2 times)*

give a bit more of, give a bit more of you. _____

1st time: softer
2nd time: even softer

(2nd time shout LOVE.)

⊕ *Coda*

A lit - tle bit more of, ___ a lit - tle bit more of ___ love. _

I Am Proud
to Be an American

Proud to Be an American

Words and Music by Carmino Ravosa

Solo (1st time), Chorus (2nd time)

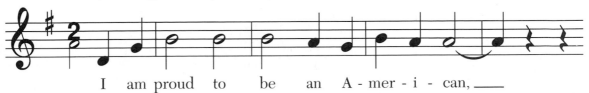

I am proud to be an A-mer-i-can, _____

A-mer-i-can, _____   A-mer-i-can. _____

I am proud to be an A-mer-i-can, _____

Fine

A-mer-i-can, _____   that's   me. _____

I'm proud   of   this coun-try,   proud   of   this   land.

D.C.

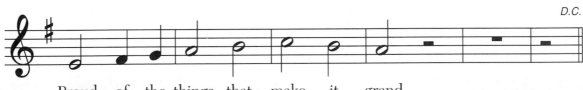

Proud   of   the things   that   make   it   grand.

READING

This section of your book will show you
how to read notes and rhythm.

Won't it be fun to be able to sing at sight!

You will learn solfa syllables— *do, re, mi, so, la*.
Each syllable stands for one note.
You will begin with simple chants,
like thc ones you say on the playground.

Before long you'll be able to look at a song
and know how it will sound before you sing it.

Reading music, like reading words,
helps us understand even more
about music.

section 3

213

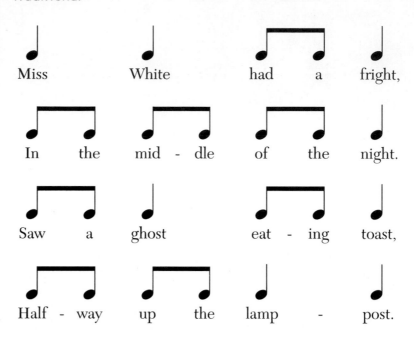

Miss White Had a Fright

Traditional

Miss White had a fright,
In the mid - dle of the night.
Saw a ghost eat - ing toast,
Half - way up the lamp - post.

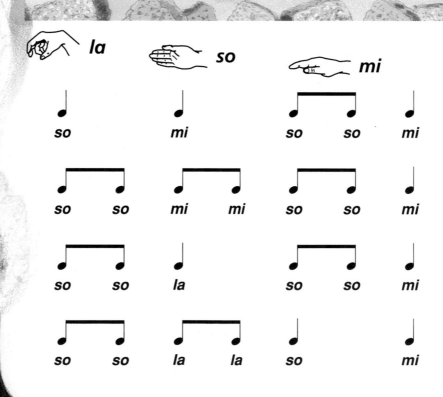

la   so   mi

so   mi   so   so   mi

so   so   mi   mi   so   so   mi

so   so   la   so   so   mi

so   so   la   la   so   mi

Singing LA, SO, MI

Bobby Shafto

Old Nursery Song

© The Kodály Context. (Choksy) Published by Prentice-Hall, Inc., 1981

 la

 so

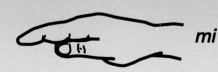 mi

Rain, Rain

Street Rhyme

Rain, rain, go a - way,

Come a - gain some oth - er day.

so mi so la so mi la
so _____

so la mi la so la mi
so _____

216

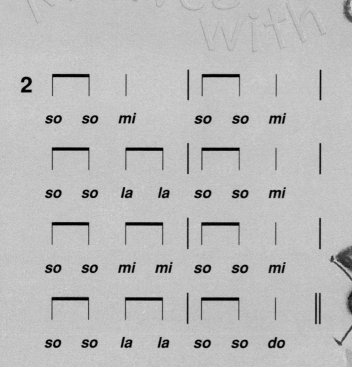

2

so so mi   so so mi

so so la la so so mi

so so mi mi so so mi

so so la la so so do

How many motives are in the music above?
Are any of the motives exactly alike?

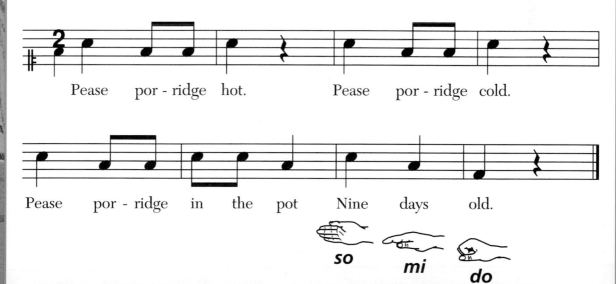

Pease Porridge Hot

Mother Goose Rhyme

Pease   por - ridge   hot.   Pease   por - ridge   cold.

Pease   por - ridge   in   the   pot   Nine   days   old.

so   *mi*   *do*

217

"Bounce High, Bounce Low" as Two Motives

Show the motives as you sing "Bounce High, Bounce Low."
Pat the beat on your legs as you sing
"Bounce High, Bounce Low" using rhythm syllables.
How many beats are in each motive?

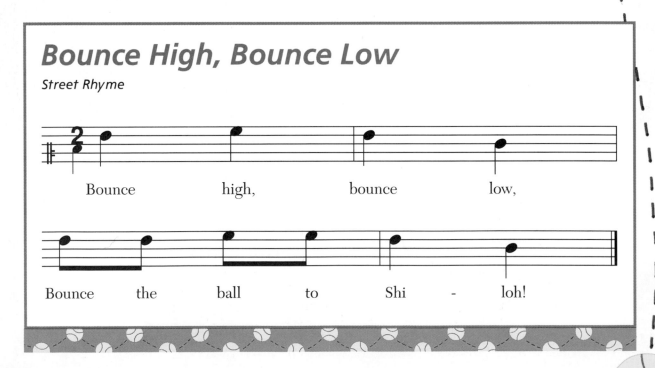

Bounce High, Bounce Low
Street Rhyme

Bounce high, bounce low,

Bounce the ball to Shi - loh!

Rocky Mountain

Southern Folk Song

1. Rocky mountain, rocky mountain, rocky mountain high;

   When you're on that rocky mountain, hang your head and cry!

   Refrain:

   Do, do, do, do, Do remember me;

   Do, do, do, do, Do remember me.

2. Sunny valley, sunny valley, sunny valley low;

   When you're in that sunny valley, sing it soft and slow. *Refrain*

3. Stormy ocean, stormy ocean, stormy ocean wide;

   When you're on that deep blue sea, There's no place you can hide. *Refrain*

Phrases and Ostinatos

Here Comes a Bluebird

Words Adapted by Jill Trinka   Traditional

Here   comes   a   blue - bird   in   through my   win - dow,

Hey, _____ diddle dumma day   day   day. ____

Take   a   lit - tle   part - ner,   Tap him   on   the   shoul - der,

Hey, _____ diddle dumma day   day   day. ____

A Two-Part Rhythm

220

Form

Can you clap the rhythm of these words?

Rocky Mountain

Southern Folk Song

1. Rocky mountain, rocky mountain,
   rocky mountain high;
   When you're on that rocky mountain,
   hang your head and cry!

   Refrain:
   Do, do, do, do, Do remember me;
   Do, do, do, do, Do remember me.

2. Sunny valley, sunny valley,
   sunny valley low;
   When you're in that sunny valley,
   sing it soft and slow.
   Refrain

3. Stormy ocean, stormy ocean,
   stormy ocean wide;
   When you're on that deep blue sea,
   There's no place you can hide.
   Refrain

Find the Long Sounds

Are You Sleeping?

Folk Song from France

2

Are   you   sleep - ing,   are   you   sleep - ing,

Bro - ther   John, ___   Bro - ther   John? ___

Mor - ning   bells   are   ring - ing,   mor - ning   bells   are   ring - ing.

Ding,   ding,   dong ___   Ding,   ding,   dong. ___

First Way

Second Way

2

Bow wow wow

Whose dog art thou?

Lit - tle Tom-my Tuck-er's dog,

Bow wow wow.

2

Bow wow wow ____

Whose dog art thou? ____

Lit - tle Tom-my Tuck-er's dog,

Bow wow wow. ____

Can you guess what song this is?

so mi do mi do mi so
do _____

so la so mi so so do
do _____

I See the Moon

Words by Earl Rogers   Traditional

I   see   the   moon   and   the   moon   sees   me;

God   bless   the   moon   and   may   God   bless   me.

From LET'S SING TOGETHER by Denise Bacon. © 1971 by Boosey & Hawkes.

Let's Meet the Half Note

Yellow Bird

Traditional Folk Game

2 Yel - low bird, yel - low bird, through my win - dow,

Oh John - ny I'm tired. _____

A Three Note Pattern

I Bought Me a Cat
Folk Song from the United States

I bought me a cat,

And the cat pleased me.

I fed my cat under

Yonder tree.

Cat goes fiddle-i-fee.

Hen goes chimmy-chuck.

Duck goes quack, quack.

Goose goes hissy, hissy.

Read a Rhythm

Listen for this rhythm pattern in the music:

What happens to the beat in this piece?

"In the Hall of the Mountain King"
from *Peer Gynt Suite, No. 1*........Grieg

A New Note

Listen for the new note.

Old MacDonald

Old MacDonald had a farm, E-I-E-I-O,
And on this farm he had some:

Singing with RE

Sing with *re*
for the new sound.

Bow Wow Wow

Traditional Nursery Song

2 | | || ⵣ |
  d   *d*   *d*
  Bow   wow   wow,

| | || ⵣ |
m   *m* *m* *m*
Whose dog art thou?

s *s* *s* *l* *s* *m* *d*
Lit - tle Tom - my Tuck-er's dog,

| | || ⵣ ||
m   *r*   *d*
Bow   wow   wow.

An Old Friend

Knock the Cymbals

Traditional

2

d m s m m m

Knock the cym-bals, do, oh, do.

d m s m r m r

Knock the cym-bals, do, oh, do.

d m s m m m

Knock the cym-bals, do, oh, do.

l l s m d d

Hel - lo, Su - san Brown - o.

When *do* is in space 1:

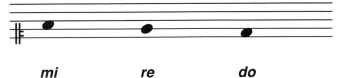

mi   **re**   **do**

When *do* is on line 2:

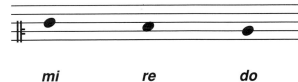

mi   **re**   **do**

When *do* is on the ledger line below the staff:

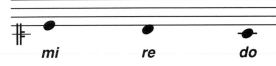

mi   **re**   **do**

Read *mi-re-do* on the staff.

Hot Cross Buns

Traditional

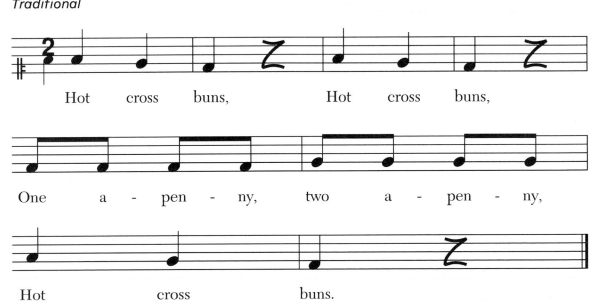

Hot   cross   buns,   Hot   cross   buns,

One   a - pen - ny,   two   a - pen - ny,

Hot   cross   buns.

Lines and Spaces

Can you see that *mi* and *do* are in spaces?

When *mi* and *do* are in spaces, *re* is always on the line between them.

Pumpkin, Pumpkin
Traditional

Pump - kin, pump - kin, round and fat,

Turn in - to a jack - o' - lan - tern just like that!

© From THE SONG GARDEN by Carol Quimby Heath. Published by the Kodaly Musical Training Institute. Used by permission.

When *mi* and *do* are on lines, *re* is in the space between them.

Pumpkin, Pumpkin
Traditional

Pump - kin, pump - kin, round and fat,

Turn in - to a jack - o' - lan - tern just like that!

© From The Song Garden by Carol Quimby Heath. Published by the Kodaly Musical Training Institute. Used by permission.

Reading in Solfa

Let's read *mi*, *re*, and *do* in solfa.

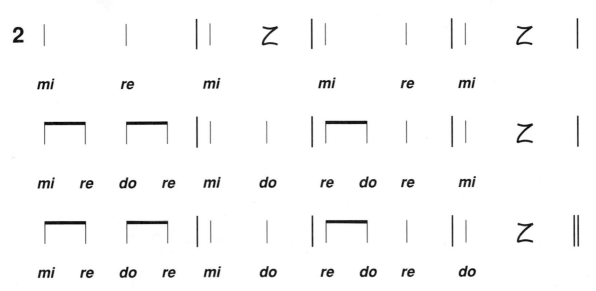

2								Z							Z	

mi   re   mi   mi   re   mi

mi re do re mi do re do re mi

mi re do re mi do re do re do

Starting on *do*

do   re   mi

Practicing RE

Frosty Weather

Game Song from Ireland

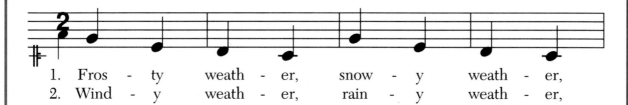

1. Fros - ty weath - er, snow - y weath - er,
2. Wind - y weath - er, rain - y weath - er,

when the wind blows, we all go to - geth - er,

The SO-MI-RE-DO Family

Show "Frosty Weather" on your hand

• starting with third space *so*.   • starting with fourth line *so*.

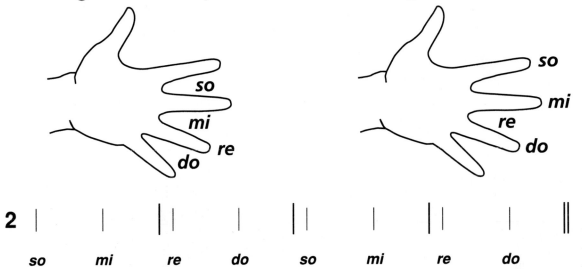

How are the first two measures
of "Frosty Weather" and
"Let Us Chase the Squirrel" different?
How are they alike?

Let Us Chase the Squirrel
Words and Music by Annie L. Preston

Let us chase the squir - rel, Up the hick - 'ry, down the hick - 'ry,

Let us chase the squir - rel, Up the hick - 'ry tree.

Let Us Chase the Squirrel
Words and Music by Annie L. Preston

Let us chase the squir - rel, Up the hick-'ry, down the hick-'ry, tree.

A New Song Two Ways

Jim-Along, Josie

Folk Song from Oklahoma

Version 1

1. Hey, jim a - long, jim a - long Jo - sie,
2. Walk, jim a - long, jim a - long Jo - sie,

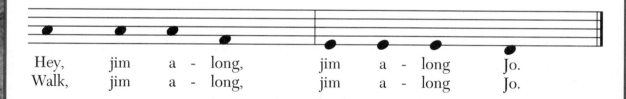

Hey, jim a - long, jim a - long Jo.
Walk, jim a - long, jim a - long Jo.

Jim-Along, Josie

Folk Song from Oklahoma

Version 2

1. Hey, jim a - long, jim a - long Jo - sie, jim a - long Jo.
2. Walk, jim a - long, jim a - long Jo - sie, jim a - long Jo.

Christmas Day Is Come

Traditional Carol from Ireland

1. Christ - mas Day is come; ___

Let us now re - joice.

Bring your flute and trum - pet,

Bring your ___ fife and drum.

Clap this ostinato as you sing.

Where Is the Ostinato?

Santa's Arrival

Music by Zoltán Kodály

do re mi so la

All the world is dressed in white,

fin - ger tips are ting - ling;

Fath - er Christ - mas comes to - night,

Rein - deer bells are jing - ling.

2. Soon across the lake he'll go,
   on his sleigh a-riding,
   Speeding over ice and snow,
   hear the runners gliding.

3. Crackling logs and mistletoe,
   red the holly berry,
   Santa Claus is coming here,
   red his face and merry.

4. Welcome then, dear Santa Claus,
   welcome then and rightly,
   Rest your star upon our tree,
   so it shines out brightly.

How Does It End?

All Around the Buttercup

Traditional Singing Game

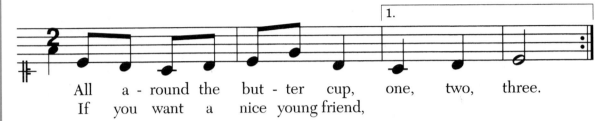

All a-round the but-ter cup, one, two, three.
If you want a nice young friend,

just choose me.

From LET'S SING TOGETHER (Bacon), Published by Boosey & Hawkes © 1971

Bye, Bye, Baby

Appalachian Lullaby

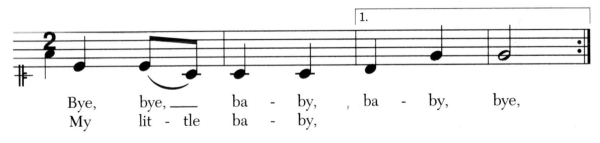

Bye, bye, __ ba - by, ba - by, bye,
My lit - tle ba - by,

ba - by, bye.

From ENGLISH FOLK SONGS, collected by Cecil Sharp. Courtesy of Oxford University Press.

Using Ledger Line DO

Suo Gan

English Words by Jill Trinka   *Lullaby from Wales*

do   re   mi

Su - o gan, do not weep,

Su - o gan, go to sleep,

Su - o gan, Moth - er's near,

Su - o gan, have no fear.

What do you notice about the rhythm
of each line?
How does the melody for each line begin?
Does the melody for each line end the same?
Which lines have the same ending?
What is the form of "Suo Gan"?

When I'm Dancing

English Words by Patricia Brewer   Music by Zoltán Kodály

1. When I'm danc-ing in my row, heel and toe,
    I   am   sing-ing   so - mi - re,   do - re - do.

2. Dance together one by one, two by two.
    When the music calls to me, calls to you.

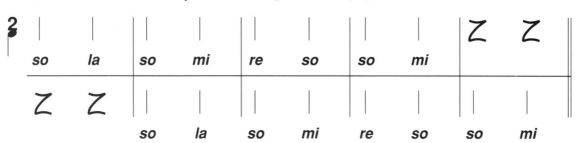

Tap the bottom rhythm. Sing the top part.

											Z	Z
so	la	so	mi	re	so	so	mi		

Z	Z										
		so	la	so	mi	re	so	so	mi

						Z			Z		–
so	la	so	mi		so	do		

–							Z			Z	
	so	la	so	mi		so	do

– = Z Z

Bow Wow Wow

Traditional Nursery Song

1.

Bow   wow   wow!

2.

Whose   dog   art   thou?

Lit - tle   Tom - my   Tink - er's   dog,

Bow   wow   wow!

 A Very Tall House

Great Big House

Folk Song from Louisiana

Great big house in New Or - leans,
Ev - 'ry room that I've been in,

1.

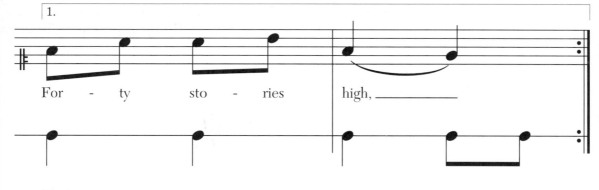

For - ty sto - ries high, _____

2.

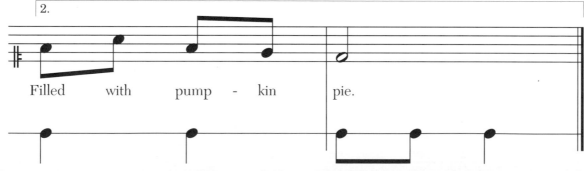

Filled with pump - kin pie.

A DUET

Button, You Must Wander

Traditional Game Song

I But - ton, you must wan - der, wan - der, wan - der,

II Wan - der, But - ton,

I But - ton, you must wan - der ev - 'ry - where;

II Wan - der, But - ton;

I Bright eyes will find you, sharp eyes will find you,

II Bright eyes find you,

I But - ton, you must wan - der ev - 'ry - where.

II Wan - der, But - ton!

Notes with Flags

Knock the Cymbals

Traditional

Knock the cym - bals, do, oh, do;

1.

Knock the cym - bals, do, oh, do;

2.

Hel - lo Su - san Brown - O.

From SWING AND TURN: TEXAS PLAY-PARTY GAMES by William A. Owens.
Copyright 1936 by Tardy Publishing Company. Reprinted by permission of McIntosh & Otis, Inc.

Ostinato:

Sing a Canon

Little Spider

English Words by Jean Sinor   *Children's Song from Hungary*

1. Lit - tle spi - der spins all day, _____
2. Then the web is fin - 'lly done, _____

Spins while all the oth - ers play; _____
Shin - ing in the morn - ing sun. _____

Singing DO-MI-SO-LA

Rocky Mountain

Folk Song from the Southern United States

Rock - y moun-tain, rock - y moun-tain, rock - y moun-tain high;

When you're on that rock - y moun-tain, hang your head and cry!

REFRAIN

Do, do, do, do, Do re - mem - ber me;

Do, do, do, do, Do re - mem - ber me.

2. Sunny valley, sunny valley,
   sunny valley low;
   When you're in that sunny valley,
   Sing it soft and slow. *Refrain*

3. Stormy ocean, stormy ocean,
   stormy ocean wide;
   When you're on that deep blue sea,
   There's no place you can hide. *Refrain*

A Jazzy Little Rhythm

Somebody Loves Me

Words and Music by Gaynor Jones

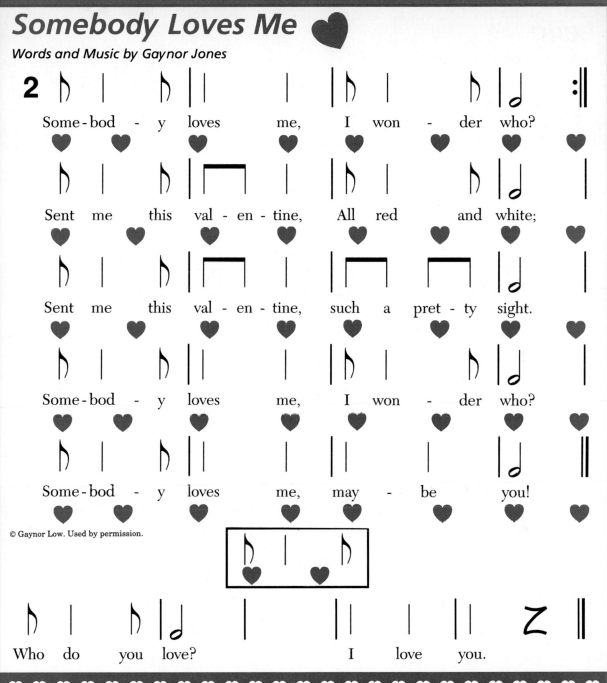

© Gaynor Low. Used by permission.

 "Largo" from *Symphony No 9*, "From the New World" (excerpt) ....Dvořák

Leila

Folk Song from North Carolina

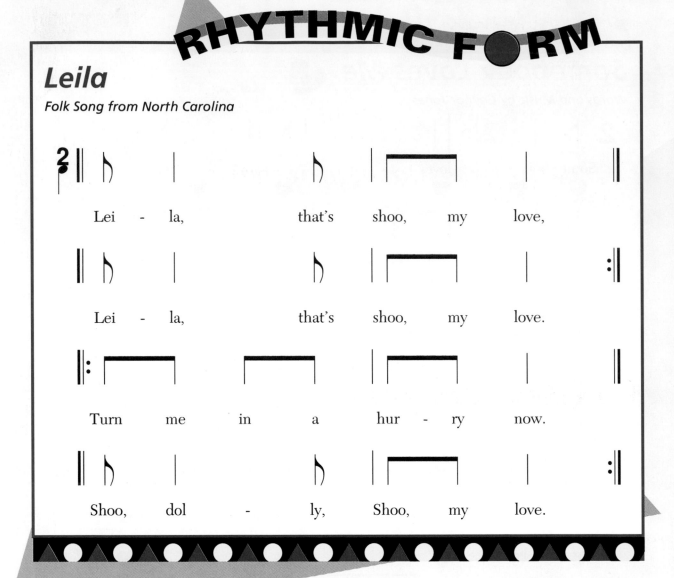

Lei - la,   that's   shoo,   my   love,

Lei - la,   that's   shoo,   my   love.

Turn   me   in   a   hur - ry   now.

Shoo,   dol -   ly,   Shoo,   my   love.

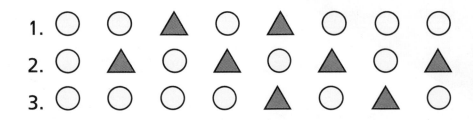

Look at the symbols ◯ and ▲ .

Each stands for two measures of the song.
Which is the best picture of the rhythmic form
of "Leila"?

1. ◯ ◯ ▲ ◯ ▲ ◯ ◯ ◯

2. ◯ ▲ ◯ ▲ ◯ ▲ ◯ ▲

3. ◯ ◯ ◯ ◯ ▲ ◯ ▲ ◯

A Rhythm Duet

Clap the bottom rhythm as you sing.

A Pretty Girl *(Una muchacha)*

Folk Song from Puerto Rico

2

Give me   a   girl   and   then   a   gui - tar   and
U - na   mu - cha - cha,   u - na   gui - ta - rra,

then   I   can   sing   my   song,   oh!
pa - ra   po - der   can - tar,   ¡ay!

Give me   a   girl   and   then   a   gui - tar   and
U - na   mu - cha - cha,   u - na   gui - ta - rra,

then   I   can   sing   my   song,   oh!
pa - ra   po - der   can - tar,   ¡ay!

MAKING UP VERSES

Dog and Cat

Folk Song from South Carolina

VERSE

1. *Bought* me a *dog, bought* me a *cat,*
   They both *fight* but *do* not *mind* that.

REFRAIN

Hi - ho,   my   dar - lin'.

2. Bought me a , bought me a ,
   They don't fit but do not mind that,
   Hi-ho, my darlin'.

3. Bought me a , bought me a ,
   They don't work but do not mind that,
   Hi-ho, my darlin'.

4. Bought me a , bought me a
   They both squeak but do not mind that,
   Hi-ho, my darlin'.

From FOLK SONGS OF THE SOUTHERN APPALACHIANS by Cecil Sharp. Used courtesy of Oxford University Press.

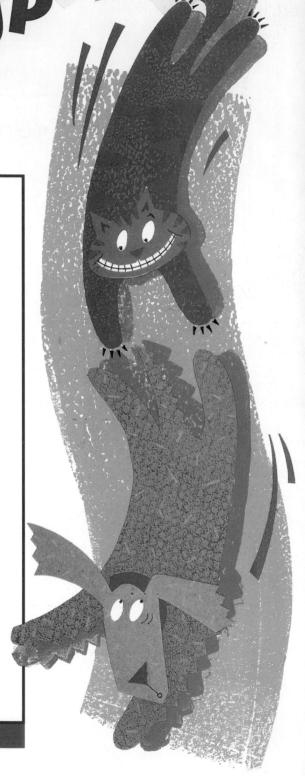

Can you make up some more verses?

Another Song About Noah

Old Ark

African American Spiritual

1. Old Ark, she reel, Old Ark she rock
Old Ark a-sit-tin' on the moun-tain top.

REFRAIN

Old Ark a-mov-in', mo-vin'
child-ren won't you come a-long,
Old Ark a-mov-in', I thank God,
Old Ark she reel, Old Ark she rock,
Old Ark a-sit-tin' on the moun-tain-top!

Fine

2. God called Noah from the mountain top,
Command Old Noah to build his ark.

3. God told Noah by the rainbow sign,
No more water but fire next time.

Canoe Song

Words and Music by Margaret E. McGhee

My pad - dle's keen and bright,

Flash - ing with sil - ver,

Fol - low the wild goose flight,

Dip, dip, and swing.

Painted Ghost Dance Shield   *Sioux*

READING AN OFF-BEAT PATTERN

My Owlet
Kiowa Indian Lullaby

Owl - et,   my   owl - et   is   sleep   -   ing

Wee   stars   are   twink - ling _____   in   the   sky
Moth - er   is   sing - ing _____   lul - la - by.

From SAIL AWAY by E. Locke. © 1988 by Boosey & Hawkes, Inc. Used by permission.

Golliwog's Cakewalk ....Debussy

Come Out Tonight

Folk Song From Alabama

<
Al - a - bam-a   gal won't you   **<** come out to   night?

<
Come out to   night?,   **<** Come out to   night?

<
Al - a - bam-a   gal won't you   **<** come out to   night and

<
dance by the   light of the   **<** moon?

THE WHOLE NOTE

o = One sound that lasts for four beats.

Hush, Hush

Traditional Spiritual

1.
1. Hush,   hush,   some-bod - y's   call - in'   my   name;

2.
Hush,   hush,   some-bod - y's   call - in'   my   name;

3.
Hush,   hush,   some-bod - y's   call - in'   my   name;

4.
Hush,   hush,   some-bod - y's   call - in'   my   name.

2. Who, who, who Lord is callin' my name? *(4 times)*

3. You, you, you Lord are callin' my name. *(4 times)*

From LET'S SING TOGETHER by Denise Bacon. © Boosey and Hawkes, 1972

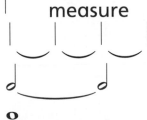

4 = Four beats in each measure

Conducting in 4/4

Conduct as you sing.

Come Out Tonight

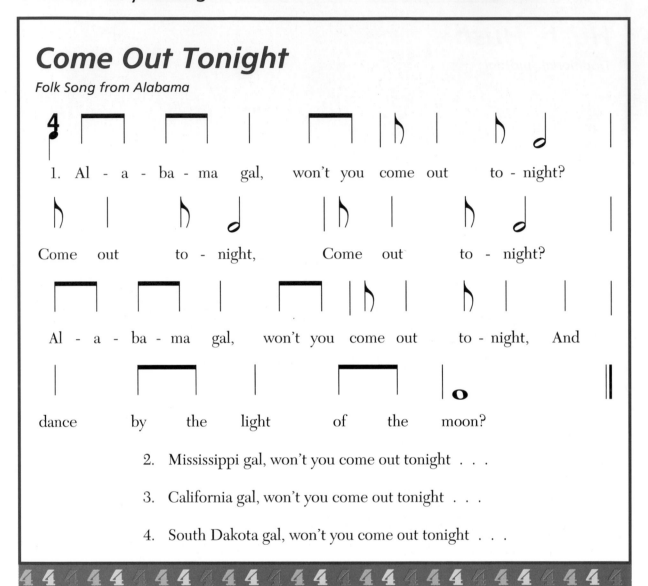

Folk Song from Alabama

1. Al - a - ba - ma gal, won't you come out to - night?

Come out to - night, Come out to - night?

Al - a - ba - ma gal, won't you come out to - night, And

dance by the light of the moon?

2. Mississippi gal, won't you come out tonight . . .

3. California gal, won't you come out tonight . . .

4. South Dakota gal, won't you come out tonight . . .

What state do you live in?
Sing about your state.

What states are next to
your state?
Sing about them, too.

A Snake in the Bush

do la so la do la so la
do la so la mi re do

Black Snake
Traditional

Black snake, black snake, where are you hid - ing?

Black snake, black snake, where are you hid - ing?

Black snake, black snake, where are you hid - ing?

Don't you bite _____ me!

In 2 or in 4?

Are You Sleeping?
Folk Song from France

Are you sleep - ing? Are you sleep - ing?

Bro - ther John? Bro - ther John?

Morn-ing bells are ring - ing, morn-ing bells are ring - ing,

Ding, dong, ding. Ding, dong, ding.

Are You Sleeping?
Folk Song from France

Are you sleep - ing? Are you sleep - ing?

Bro - ther John? Bro - ther John?

Morn-ing bells are ring - ing, morn-ing bells are ring - ing,

Ding, dong, ding. Ding, dong, ding.

A Song in Meter in 4

How Long the Train Been Gone?

African American Spiritual

How long the train been gone? _____

How long the train been gone?

How long the train been gone? _____

Oh,   yes,   Lord. _____

A Canon in Meter in 4

Can you make up some words to fit this melody?

What will your song be about?

Canon

Music by Jean Sinor

A High Note

Cut the Cake
Traditional Game Song

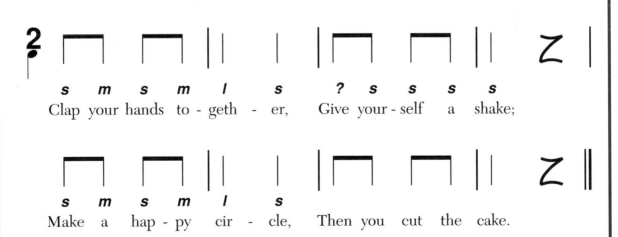

s m s m l s   ? s s s s
Clap your hands to-geth - er,   Give your-self a shake;

s m s m l s
Make a hap-py cir - cle, Then you cut the cake.

Working with High DO

Leila

Folk Song from North Carolina

d¹ s m r r m d¹ s m r r d

Lei - la,   that's shoo, my love,   Lei - la   that's shoo, my love.

1.   **2.**

Turn me in   a   hur - ry now, Shoo, dol - ly, shoo, my love,   shoo, my love.

High DO (D') on the Staff

 do

 la

so

mi

re

do

Can you find high *do* on the staff?

Can you find *do'* in this song?

Yellow Bird

Traditional Folk Game   **Collected and Adapted by Jill Trinka**

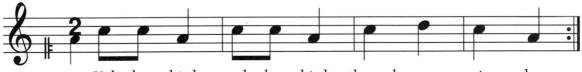

Yel - low bird,   yel - low bird,   through my   win - dow,

Oh,   John - ny, I'm   tired. _____

Another Home for High *Do*

American Gothic   *Wood*

I Want to Be a Farmer

Play-Party Song from Ohio

VERSE

I want to be a farmer, a farmer, a farmer,
I want to be a farmer, and by my lady stand.
With a pitch fork on my shoulder, my shoulder, my shoulder,
With a pitch fork on my shoulder, and a sickle in my hand.

REFRAIN

Bow   la - dies   bow,   gents,   you   know   how,
All   prom - en - ade,   all   prom - en - ade,

Swing   that   left - hand   la - dy   round,   all   prom - en - ade.

FAST and SLOW

Clocks

English Words by Polly Carder   *Traditional Danish Three-part Round*

1.

Great   big   clocks   go   tick - tock,   tick - tock.

2.

While the smal - ler man - tel clocks go   tick-tock, tick-tock, tick-tock, tick-tock,

3.

And   the   shin - y   lit - tle watch-es   keep   on   work-ing   day   and   night   with

tick - y,   tock - y,   tick - y,   tock - y,   tick - y,   tock - y,   tick.

From *Brownie's Own Songbook* (selected and compiled by Ann Roos and Alicen White) Roos and Coe-White Associates, 220 East 19th Streeet, New York, N. Y. 10003, © 1968

A New Song With DO'

Here is a new song to sing.
It uses high *do*.

Peas in the Pot

Folk Song from North Carolina

Peas in the pot, Hoe - cake a - ba - kin';

Sal - ly in the kitch - en with her shirt - tail a - sha - kin'.

From COLLECTION OF NORTH CAROLINA FOLKLORE by Frank C. Brown. Used by permission of Duke University Press.

Can you sing this song using solfa syllables?

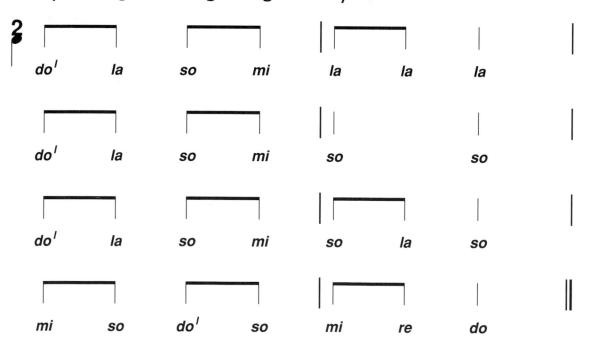

do'   la   so   mi   la   la   la

do'   la   so   mi   so   so

do'   la   so   mi   so   la   so

mi   so   do'   so   mi   re   do

Practicing High DO

My Mama's Calling Me

African American Ring Game

My ma - ma's call - ing me. You can't get out of here.

My ma - ma's call - ing me. You can't get out of here.

What shall I do? ___ Pat your { ones ___ to your knees, twos ___

Pat your threes ___ to your knees, Pat your all.

Elementary, My Dear Watson

Mystery Song

Words and Music by Gaynor Jones

© Gaynor Low. Used by permission.

Do You Know These Songs?

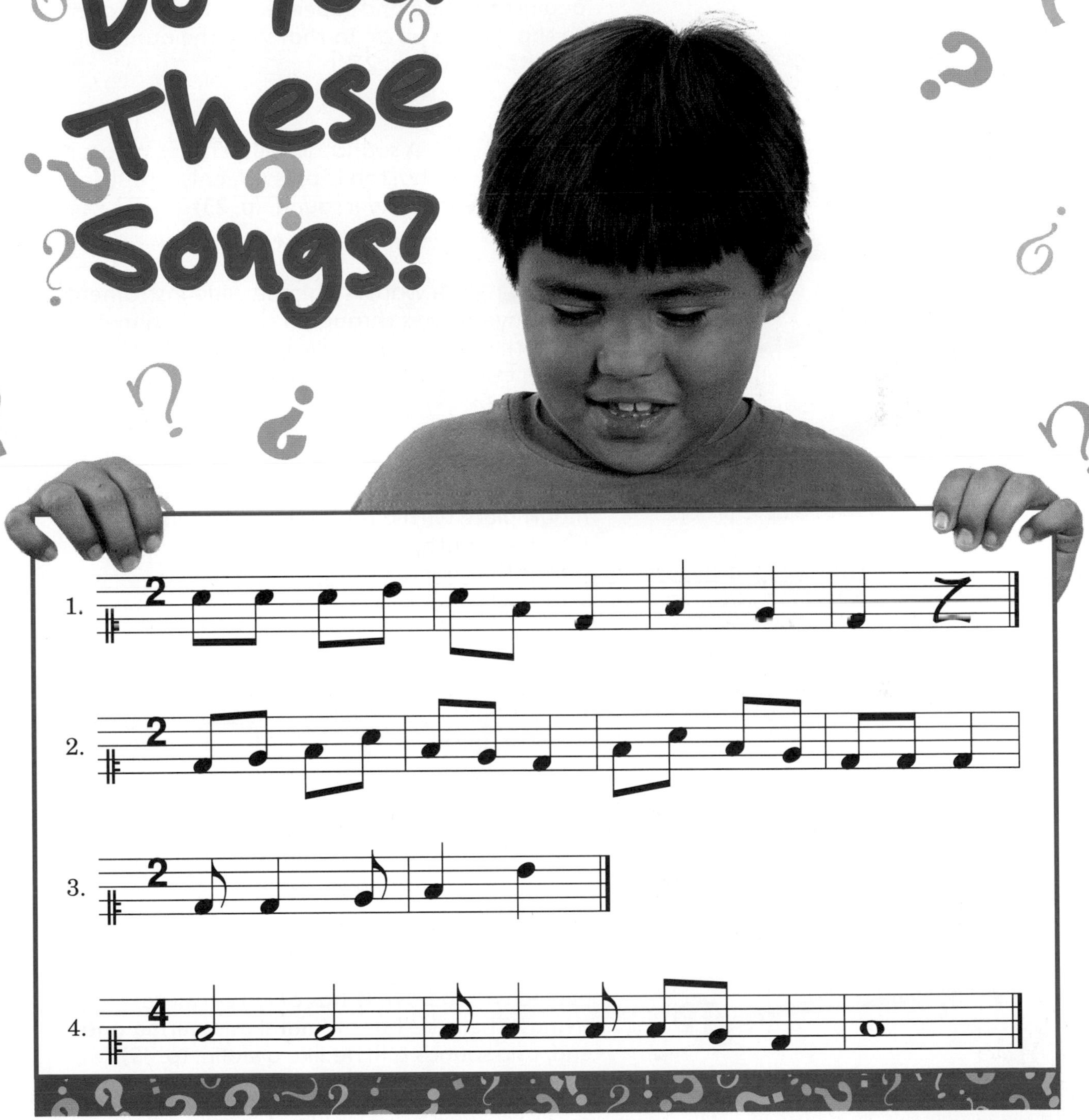

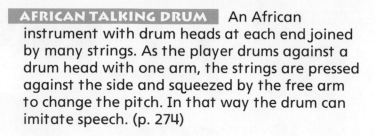

AFRICAN TALKING DRUM An African instrument with drum heads at each end joined by many strings. As the player drums against a drum head with one arm, the strings are pressed against the side and squeezed by the free arm to change the pitch. In that way the drum can imitate speech. (p. 274)

AUTOHARP A soundbox with strings across it. When a chord button is pressed, only the strings that fit the chord will sound. (p. 23)

BA WU (bah woo) A Chinese wind instrument. The player blows through a thin slit in a metal plate that covers a small square hole on the side of the instrument. The sound is like that of a clarinet. (p. 19)

CLARINET A wind instrument that has a mouthpiece with a reed. When the player blows into the mouthpiece, the reed vibrates and makes the sound. (p. 94)

DA RUAN (dah rwahn) A Chinese string instrument that is played by plucking. It has four strings and sounds like the bass strings of a guitar. (p. 19)

DULCIMER A soundbox with strings across it. The strings are usually plucked with a quill. The sound is quiet and sweet. (p. 23)

ER HU (ehr hoo) A Chinese string instrument played with a bow. It has only two metal strings. The tube has animal skin covering one end, and sounds a little like a violin. (p. 19)

FLUTE   A wind instrument shaped like a metal pipe. The player holds the flute sideways and blows across a mouthpiece. The flute can make high sounds. (p. 51)

GUITAR   A string instrument from Spain and Latin America, plucked with fingers or a pick. A guitar can play a melody. It can also play chords. Some guitars are electric. They can sound much louder. (p. 27)

KOTO   A Japanese string instrument with thirteen long strings. These are set high above the body of the instrument, which sits flat on the floor. The sound is a little like that of a harp. (p. 23)

MARACAS   Large round rattles with handles. They developed in the Carribean area and in Venezuela. Shaking the maracas makes a crisp "swishing" sound. (p. 72)

MUSICAL BOW   A string instrument found on the African continent. There are many kinds, but the one shown here has a gourd attached to make the sound larger. The sound, heard on the recording with a singer, sounds like large drops of water. (p. 23)

NATIVE AMERICAN FLUTE   A wooden, end-blown instrument. It is made from a wooden tube with part of the upper end cut out to make the sound. Finger holes along the body help the player change pitches. It sounds very much like a recorder. (p. 91)

PIANO A large keyboard instrument with strings inside. When a player presses the keys, hammers inside the piano hit the strings and make them sound. (p. 179)

PICCOLO A very small flute. It can make sounds that are higher than the flute. (p. 94)

PIPA (pee pah) A Chinese string instrument in the shape of a gourd. It has four strings and is one of the oldest of Chinese instruments. The pipa can play music in a quiet mood as well as in a loud "military style." (p. 77)

RESONATOR BELLS Metal bars that ring when struck with a mallet. Bells come in different sizes to play higher and lower sounds. (p. 99)

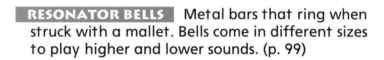

SHAKUHACHI (shah koo HAH chee) A Japanese wind instrument made of bamboo. The shakuhachi is a very well-known instrument in Japan. It is played with lots of pitch bends, clicks, and flutters. (p. 166)

SYNTHESIZER An electronic instrument with a keyboard like a piano. It uses electricity in a special way to make sound. The synthesizer can make many sounds, and imitate other instruments. (p. 11)

TAMBOURINE   A round instrument with small metal discs around the edge. Shaking or hitting the tambourine makes a jingling sound. (p. 187)

TROMBONE   A wind instrument made of brass. It makes sound the same way as the trumpet, but the pitches are lower and the player changes them by sliding a long curved tube up and down. (p. 95)

TRUMPET   A wind instrument made of brass. It has a mouthpiece shaped like a little cup. The player makes the sound by "buzzing" the lips into the mouthpiece. The trumpet can sound very loud and military. (p. 94)

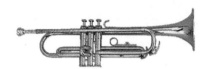

VIOLIN   A string instrument that is usually played with a bow. It can also be plucked. The violin plays sounds from low to very high. (p. 23)

WOODBLOCK   A hollow wooden bar that is hit with a mallet. It can make a ticking or popping sound. Woodblocks of different sizes make higher or lower sounds. (p. 142)

YANG QIN   (yahng chin) A Chinese string instrument. It is placed flat on a stand and played with soft mallets. Each string has another underneath. When the string above is played, the one under it vibrates, too, making a sweet, sustained sound. (p. 19)

CLASSIFIED INDEX

CLASSIFIED INDEX

SONG INDEX

ACKNOWLEDGMENTS

Credit and appreciation are due the publishers and the copyright owners for use of the following.

"Weather," by Eve Merriam. From *JAMBOREE, Rhymes for All Times* by Eve Merriam. © 1962, 1964, 1966, 1973, 1984 by Eve Merriam. Reprinted by permission of Marian Reiner.

"Willow Leaves," from *CHINESE MOTHER GOOSE RHYMES,* selected and edited by Robert Wyndham. Text © 1968 by Robert Wyndham. Reprinted by permission of Philomel Books.

PHOTOGRAPH AND ILLUSTRATION CREDITS

All photographs are by Silver Burdett Ginn (SBG) unless otherwise noted.

Cover: Mary Thalen

2: Dave Winter. 5: Martha Cooper/Viesti Associates. 8: Hiroshi Hamaya/Magnum. 9: M. Haverfield. 10–11: Michael Provost for SBG; *ill.* Kat Thacker. 12: *t.l.* Arthur Tilley/Tony Stone Images; *t.m.* © M. Tcherevkoff/Image Bank; *t.r.* Thomas Hovland/Grant Heilman; *m.m.* L. West/Bruce Coleman, Inc.; *m.t.r.* Tony Freeman/PhotoEdit; *m.r.* R. Andrew Odum/Peter Arnold, Inc.; *b.l.* SBG; *b.m.* SuperStock; *m.b.r.* John Feingersh/Uniphoto Picture Agency; *b.r.* Steve Solum/Bruce Coleman, Inc. 14–15: Rosario Valderrama. 16–17: Bryn Barnard. 18–19: James. 19: Mike Medici for SBG. 20–21: FourByFive/SuperStock. 21: *t.l.* Rosario Valderrama; *t.m.* Bryn Barnard; *t.r.* Michael Provost for SBG; *b.r.* James. 23: *t.l.* SuperStock; *t.r.* H. Oizinger/Leo de Wys, Inc.; *m.l.* Michael Provost for SBG; *b.* FourByFive/SuperStock. 24–25: Michael Provost for SBG. 26–27: John Bellissimo/LGI. 27: Bob Daemmrich/Uniphoto Picture Agency. 28–29: Victor Vaccaro. 31: Mike Medici for SBG. 32–33: Burt Glinn/Magnum. 34–35: Elliott Varner Smith for SBG. 36: Africa, Zaire, Western Kasai Province, Mweka Zone, Kuba People, Mask of a Mythic Royal Ancestor (Ngaang A Cyeem), wood, beads, cowrie shells, pigment, fabric, late 19th–early 20th century, ht. 31.1 cm, Restricted gift of the American Hospital Supply Corp., The Evanston Associates of the Woman's Board in honor of Mr. Wilbur Tuggle, Dr. and Mrs. Jeffrey Hammer, William E. Hartman, Charles A. Meyer, D. Daniel © 1993 The Art Institute of Chicago, All Rights Reserved. 40–41: Bruce Van Patter. 42–43: Kristine Bollinger. 44–45: Tony Craddock/Tony Stone Images. 46–47: © David Young-Wolff/PhotoEdit. 47: Jennifer Hewitson. 52–53: Patrick O. Chapin. 54–55: Mike Medici for SBG. 56–57: M. & E. Bernheim/Woodfin Camp & Associates. 58–59: Robert LoGrippo. 62–63: Uniphoto Picture Agency. 63: Courtesy of The John & Mabel Ringling Museum, Sarasota, Florida. 66–67: Rosario Valderrama. 68–69: Krystyna Stasiak. 70–73: Tony Stone Images. 74–75: Steven Mach. 75: Bill Smith. 76–77: © Michael S. Yamashita/Woodfin Camp & Associates. 78–79: Peggy Tagel. 79: SuperStock. 80–81: Gus Alvaras. 82–83: Bob Norieka. 84: *l.* Kevin Van Divier/Viesti Associates; *r.* © Robert Frerck/Odyssey Productions. 87: *b.r.* Martin. 88–89: Fabricio Vanden Broeck. 90–91: © 1991 George Hunter/Panoramic Stock Images. 92–93: Mike Medici for SBG. 94: Elliott Varner Smith for SBG. 96–97: Eldon Doty. 98–99: Wendy Edelson. 103: Phil Jones. 104: Will Mosgrove. 106: SuperStock. 108: Randy Verougstraete. 110: *t.* © Mark Kollowski/FPG International; *b.l.* Elliott Varner Smith for SBG; *b.m.* © Arthur Tilley/FPG International; *b.r.* Steve Dunwell/The Image Bank. 111: *t.l.* Elliott Varner Smith for SBG; *t.m.* David Young-Wolff/PhotoEdit; *t.r.* Stephen J. Krasemann/Peter Arnold, Inc.; *b.l.* © David Young-Wolff/PhotoEdit; *b.r.* © G. & V. Chapman/The Image Bank. 112: Elliott Varner Smith for SBG. 113: Mike Medici for SBG. 114–115: Cindy Rosenheim. 116–117: Bruce Van Patter. 119: Phil Borges/Tony Stone Images. 120–121: Manuel King. 122–123: Kathy Ember. 124–125: Paul Giovanopoulos. 125: Tate Gallery of Art, London/Art Resource, N.Y. 126–127: Victor Vaccaro. 128–129: Blake Thorton. 130–131: Manuel King. 132–133: Margaret Cusak. 136–137: Mike Medici for SBG; *inset p. 137* Martha Swope. 139: Gerardo Suzan. 140: Suzanne Murphy/FPG International. 141: Culver Pictures. 143: Asian Art & Archaeology/Art Resource, N.Y. 144–145: Kim Eversz. 146–147: Sarah Stone/Tony Stone Images. 148–149: Culver Pictures, Inc. 150–151: Eldon Doty. 152: © Morgan Williams/Viesti Associates. 154–155: © Rafael Macia/Photo Researchers, Inc. 156–157: John Kilgrew. 158-159: Michael Provost for SBG. 162–163: © Theo Westenberger/Gamma Liaison. 165: © 1991 Carol Rosegg/Martha Swope Associates. 166: © Guy Gillette/Photo Researchers, Inc. 168: *r.* Scala/Art Resource. 170–171: Marcos Monteiro. 172–173: Jan North. 174–175: Gary Yealdhall. 178–179: Mary Haverfield. 179: UPI/Bettmann Newsphoto. 180–181: Frank Daniel. 182–183: Wendy Edelson. 184–185: Michael Provost for SBG. 186–187: Howard Levy. 188–189: Daniel Craig. 190: John Running. 191: Tony Stone Images. 194: Flip Schulke/Black Star. 196: James. 200: Gwen Walters. 202–203: Michael Provost for SBG. 210–211: Michael Quackenbush/The Image Bank. 212–213: Christopher Morony. 214: Frank Daniel. 216–217: Kim Eversz. 218: Peggy Tagel. 219: Manfred Gottschalk/Westlight. 220–221: Wendy Edelson. 222: Randy Verougstraete. 224: Jennifer Bolton. 225: Angabe A. Schmidecker/FPG International. 226–227: Darrell Sweet. 228: *ill.* Liz Conrad; Ron Kimball Studios. 229: Liz Conrad. 230: Mike Medici for SBG. 232–233: Mary Haverfield. 234: Ron Thomas/FPG International. 235: *ill.* Kristine Bollinger. 236–237: Eldon Doty. 238: Comstock. 239: Michael Provost for SBG. 240: Bob Herger/Westlight. 241: Leo de Wys, Inc. 242–243: Dave Garbot. 244: Liz Conrad. 245: Walter Chandoha. 246: Manuel King. 247: Michael Provost for SBG. 248: Elliott Varner Smith for SBG. 249: Cezus/FPG International. 250: Thomas Kitchin/TOM STACK & ASSOCIATES. 251: Bernard Maisner. 253: © 1988 Jack Vartoogian. 254: Liz Conrad. 255: Patrick O. Chapin. 256: Dan Coffey/The Image Bank. 258: Kat Thacker. 259: John Colwell/Grant Heilman. 261: SuperStock. 263: © 1993 Comstock. 264: Jordan Coonrad. 265: Elliott Varner Smith for SBG. 266: Schneps/The Image Bank. 267: Wendy Edelson. 270: Stephanie Langley. 271: Mike Medici for SBG. 272: Scott Clemens for SBG. 273: Elliott Varner Smith for SBG.

Sound Bank Photos (in order, top to bottom) 273: The Shrine to Music Museum, University of South Dakota; SBG; Mike Medici for SBG; John Bacchus for SBG; Mike Medici for SBG; John Bacchus for SBG; Mike Medici for SBG. 275: SBG; SBG; Ken Karp for SBG; SBG; Mathers Museum; The Shrine to Music Museum, University of South Dakota. 276: SBG; SBG; Mike Medici for SBG; SBG; Ken Karp for SBG; SBG. 277: SBG; SBG; SBG; John Bacchus for SBG; SBG; Mike Medici for SBG.

Edgar Dale Media Center
O.S.U. College of Education
29 W. Woodruff Avenue
Columbus, OH 43210-1177
(614) 292-1177

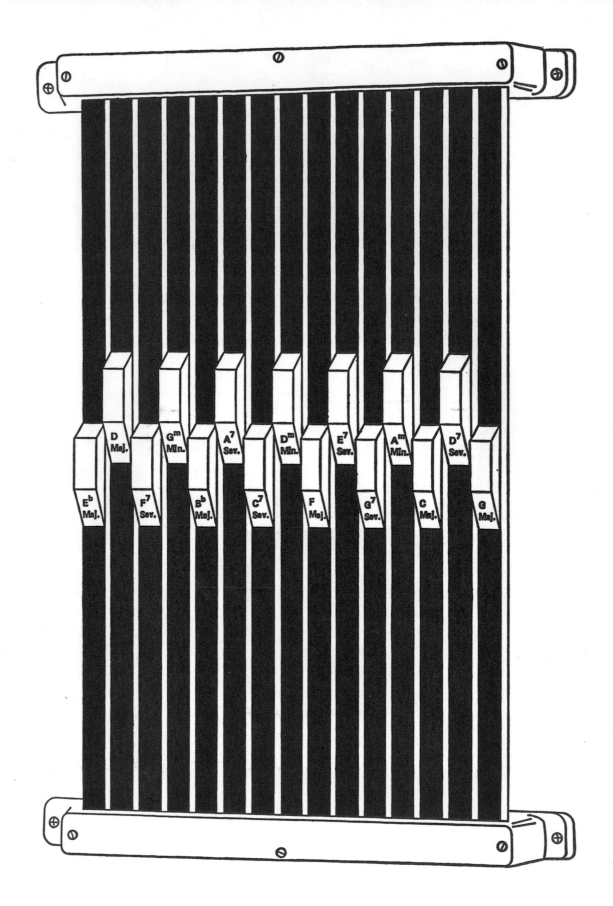